MISS LITTLEWOOD

Book, Music and Lyrics by
Sam Kenyon

||SAMUEL FRENCH||

ISBN 978-0-573-11562-2

concordtheatricals.co.uk
concordtheatricals.com

FOR AMATEUR PRODUCTION ENQUIRIES

UNITED KINGDOM AND WORLD
EXCLUDING NORTH AMERICA
licensing@concordtheatricals.co.uk
020-7054-7298

Each title is subject to availability from Concord Theatricals,
depending upon country of performance.

MISS LITTLEWOOD SONG LIST

ACT ONE

1: Prelude
2: Joan All Alone
2A: Nuns Theme
3: The Trouble With Theatre
4: My Father's Eyes
5: Paris Is a Woman
6: The Trouble With Theatre: RADA reprise
7: Joan All Alone: The Walk to Manchester reprise
8: The Wanderer's Lament
8A: Chopin Funeral March
9: Goodbye
10: The Theatre Workshop Story 1: Fuente Ovejuna
11: The Theatre Workshop Story 2: Last Edition
12: Now
13: The Theatre Workshop Story 3: Uranium 235
13A: Joan All Alone
14: Goodbye: Ormesby reprise

ACT TWO

15: In Stratford East
15A: Top of the Morning
16: A Taste of Honey: Shelagh Delaney
17: A Taste of Honey: Frank Norman reprise
18: A Taste Of Honey: Hal Prince reprise
19: Change
20: A Little Bit Of Business
21: Where Have You Been All My Life?
22: The Theatre Workshop Story 4: Oh What a Lovely War
23: Nothing Much Happened After That
24: A Decent Day

AUTHOR'S NOTE

As soon as I began researching Joan Littlewood - reading about her and interviewing former colleagues – I realised that she was a truly multi-faceted character, and decided very early on that a number of performers would serve her story best. Given that men already have the 'Seven Ages of Man' speech in *As You Like It*, I figured it was only fair to redress the balance, hence the seven Joans. They should be diverse in a number of ways – age, ethnicity, appearance, accent – and no one should be concerned about doing an impersonation. That said, Jimmie Miller (Salford) and Avis Bunnage (Chorlton-Cum-Hardy) have quite specific accents, which should be as authentic as possible. In the very first workshop reading we had only eight performers: seven women playing all the roles except for that of Gerry, played by the single man in that company. Any fully-realised production should draw on this Littlewood-inspired theatrical economy whereby, with a simple change of hat, a woman plays many parts. The set can be as basic as funds dictate, and the band a solo piano, but the music should always be played live, with any instruments as visible as possible.

Sam Kenyon, 2018

CHARACTERS

(in order of appearance)

CAROLINE EMILY – Joan's grandmother
KATE LITTLEWOOD – Joan's mother
ROBERT LITTLEWOOD – Joan's grandfather
JOAN LITTLEWOOD – sixties
JOAN 1 – young girl to young teenager
SISTER SUSANNAH – nuns, teachers
SISTER MARY
SISTER GERTRUDE
SCHOOLGIRLS
JOHN BURY GIELGUD
JOAN 2 – late teens/early twenties
SUSANNAH NICHOLSON – known as Nick – Joan's art teacher
OLDER WOMAN – Joan's paternal grandmother
PRINCIPAL OF RADA – played by Joan Littlewood herself
BEATTIE – a kindly woman en route to Manchester
JIMMIE MILLER – (later Ewan MacColl) – writer, actor, singer, songwriter
HOWARD GOORNEY – actor
ROSALIE WILLIAMS – actress
TEDDY – ASM
GERARD – actor
ALF – actor
BETSY MILLER – Jimmie's mother
JEAN NEWLOVE – choreographer and Laban expert
JOAN 3 – late twenties/early thirties
GERRY RAFFLES – actor and producer
PEARL TURNER – actress and singer
THE ARTS COUNCIL – played by Joan Littlewood herself
JOHN BURY – Designer
BARBARA YOUNG, aka PIGEON – actress
JOAN 4 – late thirties/early forties
AVIS BUNNAGE – actress
MURRAY MELVIN, aka NUT – actor
SHELAGH DELANEY – writer
FRANK NORMAN – writer
LIONEL BART – writer/composer
BARBARA (not named) – actress
VICTOR SPINETTI – actor

HAL PRINCE – director
JOAN 5 – late forties/early fifties
CEDRIC PRICE – architect of The Fun Palace
FRENCH BELLBOY
BARBARA WINDSOR – actress
JOAN 6 – late fifties
REPORTER

To
Mum

For
Dad

Because of
Murray

ACT ONE

There is a large screen above the stage, onto which various images will be projected during the show, and a year counter, currently set at 1914. A selected seat in the auditorium has a script with JACK's *lines under it.*

[MUSIC NO. 1: "PRELUDE"]

ALL WOMEN

AH, AH, AH, AH, AH, AH, AH

Scene One

The LITTLEWOOD *home: eight, Stockwell Road, London.* KATE *at the kitchen sink, vomiting into it,* CAROLINE EMILY *seated at a table.*

CAROLINE EMILY Turn around. I knew it. You little...

KATE Don't, Ma. What am I to do?

CAROLINE EMILY Too late for questions like that. How far gone are you?

KATE Nearly seven months.

CAROLINE EMILY Well it's too late for the gin cure. We could put it up for adoption, I suppose, not that anyone would want it.

KATE Stop it, Ma. You're cruel, you are.

CAROLINE EMILY Wait till your father gets home. Then you'll know cruel.

ROBERT enters.

ROBERT Well he's home, now. What's up?

KATE We're having silverside for supper.

CAROLINE EMILY Fine: Robert? Our Kate is eating for two, nowadays.

> **KATE** *is silent.* **ROBERT** *sits down slowly at the kitchen table. Tension.*

ROBERT You'll tell, or you'll be out on your ear, girl. Well?

> **KATE** *gets up and whispers into his ear, then runs upstairs.*

And now, Caroline Emily, you're going to tell me where I can find him, and I'm going to sort him out.

CAROLINE EMILY St Martin's le Grand. You'll find him in the Lord Raglan pub, most likely. His stall's round the corner.

> **ROBERT** *nods to* **CAROLINE EMILY**, *puts his boots, coat and hat back on and turns to the* **AUDIENCE**.

ROBERT You there, I want a word with you. Yes, you.

> **JOAN LITTLEWOOD** *appears and indicates the* **AUDIENCE MEMBER** *who is to play* **JACK**.

JOAN LITTLEWOOD Don't panic, darling. You'll find the script under your seat.

ROBERT Stand up. Know a girl called Kate Littlewood, do you? Goes by the name of Kitty.

JOAN LITTLEWOOD Deny it. Shake your head.

ROBERT Don't you shake your head at me, young lad. Don't you dare.

JOAN LITTLEWOOD Don't blush, whatever you do.

ROBERT You might well blush. I am Kate Littlewood's father and I am here to know your intentions.

JOAN LITTLEWOOD That's your cue.

JACK *(reading)* I'm to be married to another girl, sir.

ROBERT I see. Spineless little coward. You've made your bed, and my daughter's. Now you'll lie in it. Six shillings a week from now until the child turns sixteen. Take my offer before I double it.

JOAN LITTLEWOOD Nod.

ROBERT Now then: your business?

JACK *(reading)* Grocer, sir.

JOAN LITTLEWOOD You tell him.

ROBERT Six shillings a week, Mondays, prompt. And a tray of Williams pears on the child's birthday. The finest, you understand. You may sit down.

> **ROBERT** *nods to* **JOAN LITTLEWOOD** *who steps up on stage.* **ROBERT** *exits during the following speech.*

JOAN LITTLEWOOD So that's how I came to be. A gusset shifter down by the station, New Year's Eve 1913, and the champagne of Jack's orgasm spawned yours truly. *(To the* **AUDIENCE MEMBER***)* Thanks, darling: you've done your bit for the war effort. *(To* **AUDIENCE***)* October sixth, 1914 was my birthdate, a few months into The War To End All Wars – although, as there hasn't been a single day without war since then, it's hard not to take it personally. Kate named me Joan Maudie Littlewood. And she never forgave me. For being born, that is. I do hope, by the end of all this, that you feel somewhat differently. About time for a song, don't you think?

[MUSIC NO. 2: "JOAN ALL ALONE"]

I'M JOAN
JOAN ALL ALONE FROM MY HEAD TO MY TOES
IF NOBODY LOVES ME, WHAT DO I CARE?
AS JOAN, JOAN ALL ALONE FROM MY HEELS TO MY NOSE,
I SING TO MYSELF, AND PLAY SOLITAIRE.
BUT IF, SOMEDAY, SOMEONE SHOULD APPEAR,

SHOULD COME FROM OVER THERE
TO SOMEWHERE NEARER HERE,
I'D TELL THEM:
"NOW THAT YOU'VE MADE YOURSELF KNOWN, I'LL BE 'JOAN
    ALL ALONE' NO MORE".

Music continues under **JOAN LITTLEWOOD***'s speech.*

Now you may all be thinking: 'Joan Littlewood? Who's she when she's at home?' Well, this was not always the case. You might as well ask, 'Why do we know about so many unremarkable men and so few remarkable women?' 'A charismatic theatrical revolutionary', they called me. When we returned to the International Theatre Festival in Paris in '58 the crowd carried me into the theatre: that's how famous I was. None of this 'a-blurry-photo-of-my-arse-trended-on-Twitter-for-twelve seconds-and-now-I've-got-a-book-deal' nonsense. No. Proper 'I had that Joan Littlewood in my cab the other week' famous. One of my shows is so notorious it still pisses off the establishment. But that's for Act Two. Tonight, we're going on tour, just like in the old days, with my theatre company, only this time it's a tour of my life. The lows, the highs, how I changed the world: that sort of light-hearted stuff. And you'll meet a chap called Gerry. Nowadays this is the only place to catch sight of him. I've got a bone to pick. But for now I need a volunteer...*(underscoring ends) (To* **JOAN 1,** *planted in the* **AUDIENCE***)* You. You'd make terrific casting. Do you mind coming with me? *(To* **JOAN 1***'s audience neighbours)* I promise you can have her back in a short while.

JOAN LITTLEWOOD *and* **JOAN 1** *step onto the stage together.*

(handing **JOAN 1** *a cap)* Pop this on. Think of it as a costume. Or a weapon. There was something in the way you took your seat that caught my eye. You're perfect. You're playing me. No pressure. My advice to you, sweetheart: don't like

what you see? Do something better. Change, and the world changes with you. *(To* AUDIENCE*)* So yes: a tour. That last scene? How Not To Tell Your Parents You're Pregnant.

Musical underscoring restarts.

SISTERS SUSANNAH, MARY *and* GERTRUDE, *and* SCHOOLGIRLS *enter, carrying desks, which they begin to lay out in a grid. Year counter counts up to 1921. Music continues, morphing back into* "JOAN ALL ALONE" *in time for the reprise.*

Oh: here they come. Subtle. *(To the* CAST*)* So rude, interrupting. I can take a hint, you know. *(To* JOAN 1*)* You mustn't mind me. I'll be better with you. The rest of them drive me up the wall, sometimes, but you won't ever get the sharp end of my tongue. *(To* AUDIENCE*)* This lot are clearly itching to get on. Itching. *(To* JOAN 1*)* So listen you and I will do a bit of that song again, and then...well: here we go: –

JOAN LITTLEWOOD and **JOAN 1**
BUT IF, SOMEDAY, SOMEONE SHOULD APPEAR,
SHOULD COME FROM OVER THERE
TO SOMEWHERE NEARER HERE,
I'D TELL THEM:

JOAN LITTLEWOOD and **JOAN 1**
"NOW THAT YOU'VE MADE YOURSELF KNOWN,

JOAN 1
I'LL BE 'JOAN ALL ALONE' NO MORE".

Song ends.

JOAN LITTLEWOOD Things I Learned At School: How a School Trip Can Change Your Life.

[MUSIC NO. 2A: "NUNS THEME"]

Scene Two

A classroom. Desks are laid out in rows, with girls sitting facing away from the AUDIENCE. SISTERS SUSANNAH, MARY *and* GERTRUDE *interrupt each other throughout, indicated by /. The effect should be that of a radio being retuned. Year counter counts up to 1926 by the end of the scene.*

SISTER SUSANNAH Today, girls, we shall be learning about The Great War...

SISTER MARY ...when Great Britain and the allies stood up to the great threat to our safety and coastal/ integrity: Kaiser Wilhelm...

SISTER SUSANNAH /And when a great number of brilliant – quite brilliant/ – men

SISTER MARY /A devastating number/ of wonderful men...

SISTER GERTRUDE /of beautiful men and women laid down their lives for /each and every one of us...

ALL /Each and every one of us.

SISTER GERTRUDE If you'll turn to page one of your text books/ – you in the corner: you'll have to share – we'll start with the war's origins...

SISTER MARY /On June twenty-eighth, 1914, a nineteen-year-old Bosnian Serb named Gavrilo Princip set out with six other accomplices. Their aim? To throw a grenade/ into the car of Franz Ferdinand, the Archduke of Austria...

SISTER SUSANNAH /Shakespeare, girls. The Merchant of/ Venice...

SISTER GERTRUDE /Today, girls, we'll be dissecting an onion. Prepare/ yourselves for tears...

SISTER MARY /And now, girls, please turn to page ninety-three in your calculus/ textbook...

SISTER GERTRUDE /And now, girls, if you'll pair up, we shall make our way to the Old Vic theatre, where we shall see Mr John Gielgud take the part of /Macbeth...

SISTER SUSANNAH /Macbeth...

SISTER MARY /Macbeth, Thane of Glamis...

SISTER SUSANNAH   ...but be sure, ladies, not to mention the name of /Macbeth—

SISTER GERTRUDE AND SISTER MARY /Macbeth...

SISTER SUSANNAH —within the auspices of the theatre itself. It is considered terribly bad luck to say the name—

JOAN 1 Macbeth!

Scene Three

1926. The Old Vic Theatre: interior.

[MUSIC NO. 3: "THE TROUBLE WITH THEATRE"]

JOAN 1

I ENTER THE THEATRE
AS THOUGH IN A DREAM
FOR I'D NEVER SEEN A THEATRE FROM INSIDE
IT SMELLS OF EXPECTATION
OF PLEASURE AND DELIGHT... WHAT A NIGHT,

JOAN 1 AND JOAN LITTLEWOOD

WHAT A NIGHT!

JOAN 1

THE FIERCE AUDITORIUM
IS GOLDEN AND RED
WITH THICK VELVET CURTAINS HANGING DOWN
I LOOK UP TO THE CEILING
SEE CHERUBS TAKING FLIGHT... WHAT A NIGHT, WHAT A
    NIGHT!

THE CURTAIN, IT RISES
THE PLAY IT BEGINS
THE CAULDRON, THE WITCHES AND THE VERSE
AND I HAVE SEEN SUCH BEAUTY
YES I HAVE WITNESSED GOD
IN THE POWER AND GLORY OF THE BARD!

JOHN GIELGUD *enters, dressed as Macbeth.*

JOHN GIELGUD Is this a dagger which I see before me? *(He
    hesitates)*

JOAN 1

THEN SOMEBODY FALTERS
BUT NO ONE REACTS

JOHN GIELGUD Come, let me clutch thee!

JOHN GIELGUD *gradually exits during the following verse.*

JOAN 1

THEY JUST SAY THE LINE AND CARRY ON
THE SINGLE MOST AUTHENTIC MOMENT IN THE SHOW IS
    IGNORED
THE REST OF THE EVENING
PASSES ME BY
I FALL INTO A DIFFERENT SORT OF DREAM

JOAN 1 and **JOAN LITTLEWOOD**

WHERE I AM THE PRODUCER

JOAN 1

IT'S ME WHO CALLS THE SHOTS
WHEN SOMEBODY FALTERS IT ALTERS THE COURSE OF THE
    PLAY...

I EXIT THE THEATRE
NOW FULLY AWAKE
THE PLACE'S FORMER GLORY LEAVES ME COLD
THE GILT AND ALL THE VELVET
ARE GUILTY AS ALL HELL... I FEEL OLD

JOAN 1 and **ENSEMBLE**

I FEEL OLD!
THE TROUBLE WITH THEATRE
IS ALWAYS THE SAME
IT ISN'T JUST THE PICTURE; IT'S THE FRAME

JOAN 1

THE ENTRANCE AND THE FOYER, THE WAY THAT YOU'RE
    ADDRESSED;
THE REASON THEY'RE CALLED HOUSES? YOU ENTER AS A
    GUEST.
I LEAVE THE OLD VIC THEATRE DISTINCTLY UNIMPRESSED...

ENSEMBLE

AH

JOAN 1

AND DEPRESSED...

ENSEMBLE

AH

JOAN 1 and **JOAN LITTLEWOOD**

AND OBSESSED!

JOAN LITTLEWOOD And we're back home, once more. Number eight, Stockwell Road. How To Sabotage Your Own Birthday, With The Help Of Your Mother.

Scene Four

Saturday Morning. Eight, Stockwell Road. **CAROLINE EMILY** *and* **ROBERT** *are sitting having a cup of tea. A knock at the door. Year counter counts up to 1930.*

ROBERT Come in.

An **OLDER WOMAN** *enters, carrying a box marked 'Williams Pears', and an envelope.*

CAROLINE EMILY Oh.

OLDER WOMAN Can I see her?

ROBERT You're not to say a word to her.

OLDER WOMAN Then I'll say it to you. Today is her sixteenth birthday. This is the last year. And this *(she hands over the envelope)* is the final payment. I'll thank you to keep your word. And not to mess with my son no more.

CAROLINE EMILY stands in anger. ROBERT places a hand on her shoulder and she sits once more. The OLDER WOMAN nods, and places the pears on the kitchen table. CAROLINE EMILY exits and returns with JOAN 1. She sees the pears, then looks at the OLDER WOMAN.

JOAN 1 Hello?

The **OLDER WOMAN** *looks* **JOAN 1** *slowly up and down, then stares into her eyes. She draws breath as though to speak.* **ROBERT** *tenses.* **KATE** *enters as the* **OLDER WOMAN** *leaves.* **JOAN 1** *shrugs and picks up the pears.*

KATE I suppose the good news is, now you'll have to earn your keep like the rest of us.

ROBERT Kate. It's her birthday.

JOAN 1 Stuff you.

CAROLINE EMILY Joan!

KATE There's gratitude. I gave birth to you when I was your age.

JOAN 1 Well, days like this I wish you'd kept your maidenhood.

KATE You're just like him. Face of a peasant, pig-eyed, voice like a foghorn and a heart like flint.

JOAN 1 And you are, and always will be, a slut.

The kitchen disappears and **JOAN 1** *is in her bedroom, the pears on her lap.* **JOAN 1** *takes a mirror off her bedside table and looks at herself.*

[MUSIC NO. 4: "MY FATHER'S EYES"]

MY FATHER'S EYES
WERE DARK, LIKE MINE
HE ALSO HAD THIS GAP BETWEEN HIS TEETH
AND UNDERNEATH
APPARENTLY
WE'RE SIMILAR

MY FATHER'S VOICE
WAS DEEP, LIKE MINE
HIS FACE, LIKE MINE, WAS BROAD AND FLAT AND PLAIN
SHE CAN'T EXPLAIN
THE OTHER WAYS
WE'RE SIMILAR

OTHER GIRLS' FATHERS CHOP LOGS
OTHER GIRLS' FATHERS FIGHT FIRES
THEY DIG HOLES IN THE GROUND
OR JUST STICK AROUND

OTHER GIRLS' FATHERS CUT CLOTH
OTHER GIRLS' FATHERS MEND FENCES
THEY CLIMB CHIMNEYS, SWEEP SOOT
OR SIMPLY STAY PUT

MINE SENDS A BOX OF WILLIAMS PEARS ONCE A YEAR...

(spoken) Who does he think he is?

Sung:

ONE DOZEN PERFECT WILLIAMS PEARS ONCE A YEAR...

(spoken) Who do *I* think he is?

Sung:

MY OLD MAN IS HANDSOME
MY OLD MAN IS KIND
MY OLD MAN IS SAD HE HAD TO LEAVE ME BEHIND
MY OLD MAN IS FAMOUS
MY OLD MAN IS ALIVE
AND ONE DAY, SOME DAY, MY OLD MAN WILL ARRIVE

HE'LL SAY "JOAN, YOU'RE BRILLIANT, JOAN, YOU'RE EXCITING"
HE'LL SAY, "JOAN, YOU'VE NOTHING TO HIDE"

HE WON'T TELL ME I'M DRIVING HIM WILD
HE'LL SAY

JOAN LITTLEWOOD

" YOU'RE ALL THAT A FATHER COULD WANT IN A CHILD"

JOAN 1

AND I WILL BE MY FATHER'S PRIDE

MY FATHER'S EYES
WERE DARK, LIKE MINE

MY FATHER'S VOICE
WAS DEEP, LIKE MINE

BUT TILL I MEET THE MAN HIMSELF
I'LL SIT HERE IN MY LONELY BED
MY FATHER'S EYES ARE ONLY IN MY HEAD

Music continues as underscore.

JOAN LITTLEWOOD *(interrupting, over underscore:)* No, no. Far too self-indulgent, darling. Especially when it's your birthday. No, we can't have it like that.

KATE *(offstage)* Who are you talking to in there?

JOAN LITTLEWOOD and **JOAN 1** Myself.

JOAN LITTLEWOOD *(to* **JOAN 1***)* Tell you what, darling, why don't you go and make us both a nice cup of tea? I'll cover you. Oh, and give us that cap, would you? I'd hate for you to lose it.

JOAN 1 *hands* **JOAN LITTLEWOOD** *the cap, and exits, bemused.*

(spotting **JOAN 2***)* Little bird, come with me. Could you take over? *(Handing* **JOAN 2** *the cap)* Try it on for size. I age, after all, like any other mortal, and now is as good a time as any.

JOAN 2 *puts on the cap.*

Suits you. Now then...we're going to try that number again, only this time... *(To* **CONDUCTOR***)* Take us back a bit, please?

*(***BAND** *plays beginning of final section)* Bit further. *(...Previous section)* Yes lovely. *(To* **JOAN 2***)* Sing with me.

JOAN LITTLEWOOD *sings, conducting* **JOAN 2** *in for second line onwards:*

DA, DA, DA-DA ALIVE

JOAN 2 and **JOAN LITTLEWOOD**
AND ONE DAY, SOMEDAY, MY OLD MAN WILL ARRIVE

JOAN LITTLEWOOD Now then, this time, really give him what for.

JOAN 2
I'LL SAY, "WHERE WERE YOU WHEN I NEEDED A FATHER?"

JOAN LITTLEWOOD That's more like it!

JOAN 2
THEN I'LL SAY: "TOO LITTLE, TOO LATE"

JOAN LITTLEWOOD That's terrific!

JOAN 2
I WON'T SIMPER AND CLING TO HIS SLEEVE
I'LL SAY "MAKE SURE THE DOOR CLOSES BEHIND WHEN YOU
      LEAVE.
NOW GO AND MAKE YOUR PEACE WITH KATE."

MY FATHER'S EYES
MAY LOOK LIKE MINE
MY FATHER'S VOICE
MAY SOUND LIKE MINE
BUT HE HAS NEVER BEEN AROUND
THE ONLY WAY I KNOW HE CARES
IS WILLIAMS PEARS...

MMM underscore.

JOAN LITTLEWOOD Much better. Much more me. Now pick one of the pears. Give it a squeeze...now a sniff...and now... take a big bite!

Humming, **JOAN 2** *does the following under* **JOAN LITTLEWOOD***'s speech: holds one up, squeezes it, sniffs it, then, when instructed, bites into it with great satisfaction.*

(under playout) ...and don't forget: your art teacher, Miss Nicholson, is waiting for you in Lyons' tea rooms. Happy birthday, darling.

JOAN 2 *bites the pear to hold it and grabs her coat and scarf.* **JOAN 1** *reappears carrying a cup of tea. Song continues as underscore.*

(to **JOAN 1***)* Thanks, sparrow. Piping hot: lovely. We had to make do in your absence. Do stick around, though, won't you? I've got you in mind for a couple of other parts.

JOAN 1 What? You just sent me out to make a cup of tea.

JOAN LITTLEWOOD That's right. And you took a little longer than I'd hoped.

JOAN 1 That's how long it takes a kettle to boil.

JOAN LITTLEWOOD *(to* **AUDIENCE***)* It's called 'casting by availability'. *(To* **JOAN 1***)* I promise you I'll keep you busy.

JOAN 1 But—

JOAN LITTLEWOOD You're slowing the pace of the story. Trust me: I'm a director.

Song ends. **JOAN 1** *relents and re-enters* **AUDIENCE.**

(to **JOAN 2***)* You're on! *(To* **AUDIENCE***)* Meeting My Art Teacher at Lyons' Tea Rooms, or How To Accept An Invitation From A Probable Lesbian, Without Actually Committing To Anything.

Scene Five

In Lyons' tea rooms. NICK *and* JOAN 2 *are at a table together.*

NICK   ...I went through an existentialist phase, myself. You know: smoking like a navvy and taking moonlit riverside walks with a faintly suicidal flavour to them. So I know exactly what it's like.

JOAN 2 *sips her tea, lifts her scone.*

JOAN 2   Miss Nicholson—

NICK   Call me Nick, out of hours, Joan.

JOAN 2   Nick. It's my birthday today. Sixteen.

She grimaces, then takes a bite. NICK *raises her eyebrows, then raises her teacup.*

NICK   Then I'd like to make a toast: to you, to art, and to fruitful relationships.

They toast.

JOAN 2   Thank you.

NICK   Oh, you've nothing to thank me for, yet.

JOAN 2   I've had an audition—

NICK   Look: it's probably a silly idea, but I've just had an awfully jolly thought. It's just that, well, I'm going somewhere on holiday and I think you'd rather like it, too.

JOAN 2   Really? Where?

NICK   Oh no, that's a surprise. If you think your family would allow you, that is. I'd vouch for your safety and everything. And we could call it your birthday treat. What do you say?

JOAN 2   Er...yes?! Yes please?!

NICK Now, what were you going to say? Something about an audition?

JOAN 2 Well yes. I haven't been able to tell anyone. You see I've been offered a scholarship at the Royal Academy of Dramatic Art.

NICK The RADA? I thought we'd agreed that painting is your real talent. But listen: I do think you're awfully clever, and on holiday, of course, we'll have oodles of time to talk this sort of thing through.

JOAN 2 You still want me to come?

NICK Of course you must come. Don't be silly.

JOAN LITTLEWOOD *(to* **AUDIENCE***)* So I did. Once we'd got Robert and Carrie Em's permission, Nick told me where we were going. And it wasn't a stick of rock and a Kiss-Me-Quick postcard. No, by the light of heaven, it was PARIS!

Scene Six

Song. During the number, **JOAN 2** *and* **NICK** *travel to Paris.*

[MUSIC NO. 5: "PARIS IS A WOMAN"]

JOAN 2

THIS IS THE TRAIN
THIS IS THE TRAIN TO DOVER
THESE ARE THE FIELDS
THESE ARE THE COWS
THIS IS THE AIR
THIS IS THE AIR OF FREEDOM
BREATHE IT IN!

THESE ARE THE CLIFFS
THESE ARE THE DOVER SEAGULLS
THIS IS THE SEA
THESE ARE THE WAVES
THIS IS LA MANCHE
THIS IS THE SHORE OF FRANCE
KINGDOM COME!

Arrival in Paris.

THERE ON A TREE, A SWEET CHESTNUT FLOWER;
SOIR DE PARIS: THE SCENT OF THE HOUR;
MADELEINES IN TEA, FOR PROUST AND THE POWER OF
    MEMORY...
COFFEE, BAGUETTE, THE NOSE OF A CLARET;
LEEKS VINAIGRETTE WITH FRESH-GRATED CARROT;
MY FIRST CIGARETTE: PERFUMES OF SUCH CLARITY...
IT'S SO INTENSE...
PARIS: THE PLACE WHERE SCENTS MAKE SENSE!

	ENSEMBLE
PARIS IS A WOMAN	AH
INTELLIGENT AND BOLD	AH
PARIS IS A WOMAN	AH

SOMETHING TO BEHOLD   AH

JOAN LITTLEWOOD

LA, LA, LA, LA, LA LA, LA, LA

JOAN 2

PARIS IS A WOMAN   AH
COMPLEX BY DECREE   AH

JOAN LITTLEWOOD

LA, LA, LA, LA, LA LA, LA, LA

PARIS IS THE WOMAN I   THE WOMAN
INTEND TO BE

JOAN 2 AND ENSEMBLE

PARIS IS AN ACTRESS
BORN TO PLAY HER PART
PARIS IS AN ARTIST
DEVOTED TO HER ART

JOAN 2

PARIS IS A WRITER
ERUDITE AND FREE
PARIS IS THE WOMAN I INTEND TO BE

A balcony overlooking the Seine. **NICK** *and* **JOAN** 2 *are sitting, sharing a cigarette and a glass of wine. Song continues as underscore.*

These galleries, Nick: you only get to see them if you can pay.

NICK Oils and canvases don't come cheap, Joan.

JOAN 2 I want art for everyone. A place where anyone can come and learn anything they'd like. Pottery, French, football, you name it: there'll be a class for it. A gallery; a sports hall; a library. And free, for all ages. Sciences. Arts. For people like me.

NICK Not many people have your artistic talent, Joan. Life isn't democratic. I brought you here to inspire you.

JOAN 2 If you really believe in all the art you talk about—

NICK – which I do—

JOAN 2 Then you'll agree that paintings – well actually I don't know whether it's the paintings or the galleries – but it seems to me that there's nothing less democratic than an art gallery. If painting is going to achieve anything – at all – it must be on a scale far bigger than anything we've seen this week. The size of that wall. And just as public paintings on the sides of lorries, driving round the country on perpetual tour.

NICK I've got us a studio, Joan. I'll show you when we get back. You can paint as big as you like. The light's incredible. Chelsea.

JOAN 2 Chelsea's a foreign country to the likes of me.

NICK Not for long.

JOAN 2 Whereas the theatre—

NICK Oh, the theatre.

JOAN 2 You can take it in a lorry, round the country, if you like. A thousand people can watch.

NICK Are you talking about The Royal Academy of Dramatic sodding Art, again? I thought we'd cleared that one up.

JOAN 2 I haven't decided. *(To* AUDIENCE*)* That isn't true. I posted the acceptance letter at Dover.

NICK I'm offering you a home, Joan. For you and for your art, whatever direction it takes. Whereas this theatre business: you'll be bored within a month. Besides, with your...predicament—

JOAN 2 Predicament? What predicament? My scholarship?

NICK Your background.

JOAN 2 What?

NICK I just meant that certain people see people...like...

JOAN 2 People like me. I see. In a different light. As a predicament. Well, then they can fuck right off. *(To* **AUDIENCE***)* And so can Nick. And Chelsea can fuck off, and all.

Return to London:

THIS IS THE TRAIN
THIS IS THE TRAIN TO LONDON
THIS IS THE RAIN
THIS IS THE SMOG
PARIS HAS SHOWN
HOW TO BECOME A WOMAN

JOAN 2 AND ENSEMBLE

HOW TO BE JOAN?

ENSEMBLE

JOAN!

JOAN 2

DO IT ALONE!

[MUSIC NO. 6: "THE TROUBLE WITH THEATRE"
(RADA Reprise)]

JOAN LITTLEWOOD RADA, And How To Survive It.

*Song segues into **"THE TROUBLE WITH THEATRE"** (RADA reprise). Year counter counts to 1931.*

Scene Seven

1931. In RADA.

I WALTZ INTO RADA
THE SCHOLARSHIP GIRL
THE URCHIN WITH THAT GAP BETWEEN HER TEETH
I'M NORA AND ELIZA;
CORDELIA AND KATE:
I CAN'T WAIT, I CAN'T WAIT

I HEAD FOR THE CLOAKROOM
IT'S STUFFY AND FULL
OF DEBUTANTES: AMERICAN AND BLITHE
THEY'RE HERE TO CHANGE THEIR ACCENTS
I'M HERE TO CHANGE MY FATE
I CAN'T WAIT, I CAN'T WAIT

BUT LESSONS ARE USELESS, AND TEACHERS ARE SNOBS
THEY TRAIN US UP IN VANITY, NOT ART
THEY TEACH US TO DECLAIM
IN A DOUBLET AND HOSE WITH A SWORD
MY NAME IS TOO COMMON
MY VOICE IS TOO DEEP

JOAN LITTLEWOOD *enters as* **PRINCIPAL***. Year counter counts up to 1932.*

PRINCIPAL Miss Littlewood. It would be remiss of me not to congratulate you on your recent successes: your Cleopatra, which graced the airwaves of the BBC World Service, and the verse prize awarded to you by the eminent Archie Harding—

JOAN 2 *(to* **AUDIENCE***)* Archie Harding: as rich as he is left-wing. A caviar communist, if you will. Banished by the BBC to Manchester for being too interesting. *(To* **PRINCIPAL***)* You were saying?

PRINCIPAL Each RADA graduate receives one of two letters: The West End letter, or the Regional Repertory letter. The West End letter is the revered one, obviously.

JOAN 2 *(to* AUDIENCE*)* Obviously.

PRINCIPAL And I would be confident in providing you with such a letter. In fact, I envisage you being quite at home on the West End stage, despite your predicament.

JOAN 2 At home? There? No.

PRINCIPAL It would be unprecedented for an actress to request a regional repertory letter.

JOAN 2 Neither, then. I'll make my own way.

JOAN 2 *goes to leave.*

PRINCIPAL I should tell you that it would also be unprecedented for an actress to leave the RADA without graduating.

JOAN 2 Well I'm shattering precedent after precedent this morning, aren't I, principal? I've learnt a great deal here: how to eat my sandwiches in the lavatory in order to avoid bullying by my vapid peers; how an actress with a well-turned ankle is more highly prized than one with a well-turned phrase, and that – more often than not – the offer of a home is a poisoned chalice.

JOAN 2 and ENSEMBLE
THE TROUBLE WITH RADA...

JOAN 2
WELL, WHERE DO I START?
THE SYSTEM, OR THE CHRONIC LACK OF ART?

	ENSEMBLE
THE DEBUTANTES AND POSERS	OOH
WHO THINK IT'S JUST A GAME?	
THE TEACHERS WHO INSPIRE IT: ARE THEY THE ONES TO BLAME?	OOH BLAME
I CLOSE THE DOOR ON RADA	OOH

```
WITH SOMETHING TO          AAH
     RECLAIM
AND AN AIM                 AAH
```

AND MY NAME!

PRINCIPAL Where will you go?

JOAN 2 America! Well, Manchester first, to see how Archie Harding's getting on.

JOAN LITTLEWOOD How will you get there?

JOAN 2 I'll walk.

JOAN LITTLEWOOD *(removing* **PRINCIPAL***'s hat)* Of course you will. Don't forget to be earth-shattering, will you? *(To* **AUDIENCE***)* How To Get To Manchester On A Budget.

Scene Eight

MUSIC *starts. The* COMPANY *tells the story of* JOAN 2*'s journey to Manchester in the manner of a silent movie.* JOAN 2 *carries a stick with a knapsack at its end, like Dick Whittington.* JOAN 2 *walks out of London, singing.*

[MUSIC NO. 7: "THE WALK TO MANCHESTER"] – Reprise: The Walk to Manchester

JOAN 2 and ENSEMBLE

I WALK, WALK ALL THE WAY TO MANCHESTER AS LONDON
   FALLS BEHIND
I WALK, WALK ALL THE WAY TO MANCHESTER WITH FREEDOM
   ON MY MIND
AND IF I FEEL A JOLT OF TREPIDATION AT MY FUTURE ACROSS
   THE SEA
I SAY: "WELL IF IT'S GOOD ENOUGH FOR CHARLIE CHAPLIN,
   THEN IT'S GOOD ENOUGH FOR ME!"

MUSIC *continues as underscore. Exhausted,* JOAN 2 *lies down to sleep. She is now at Burton-on-Trent. A* CROWD *appears, fearful that* JOAN 2 *is dead.* BEATTIE *steps forward and takes* JOAN 2 *into her home.* JOAN 2 *falls asleep once more.* BEATTIE *goes through* JOAN 2*'s knapsack, finds the note with* ARCHIE HARDING*'s address on it, and writes him a letter. The* COMPANY *conveys the letter to* ARCHIE HARDING, *who steps forward with a letter of his own.*

ARCHIE *(reading)* Dear Miss Littlewood, I received a letter from a Beattie of Burton-on-Trent, who tells me you've stopped off there en route to visiting us at the BBC. I had already warned everyone here about your Cleopatra, which they will insist on hearing - for a fee, of course. I would also adore it if you'd write a piece about your odyssey. It will strike some chords, light some fires, and earn you another fee. Hurry there's a chap I'd like you to meet. Funds enclosed; I regard myself in your corner. Archie Harding

The COMPANY *conveys* ARCHIE HARDING*'s letter to* JOAN 2, *who immediately boards a train to Manchester.*

JOAN 2 and ENSEMBLE

> I TAKE THE STEAM TRAIN UP TO MANCHESTER AS BURTON FALLS BEHIND
> I TAKE THE STEAM TRAIN UP TO MANCHESTER WITH FREEDOM ON MY MIND
> AND IF I FEEL A JOLT OF TREPIDATION AT THE WORLD OF THE BBC
> I SAY: "WELL IF IT'S GOOD ENOUGH FOR ARCHIE HARDING, THEN IT'S GOOD ENOUGH FOR ME!"

JOAN 2 *arrives in Manchester to be greeted by paparazzi. We see headlines: "Stockwell urchin walks to Manchester!" "RADA dropout claims Chaplin's her inspiration!" etc. Year counter counts up to 1933.*

Scene Nine

The canteen of the BBC in Manchester. **JIMMIE MILLER**
sings with his hand cupping one ear. **JOAN 2** *stands
and watches.*

JOAN LITTLEWOOD Meeting Jimmie Miller in the BBC canteen,
Manchester. How Politics Can Be an Aphrodisiac.

[MUSIC NO. 8: "THE WANDERER'S LAMENT"]

JIMMIE MILLER
SHE SAID SHE'D LOVE ME HANDSOMELY UNTIL MY TIME WAS
    DONE
WITH BREATH AND HEART AND BODY AND THE RISING
    ROILING SUN
SHE SAID SHE'D TREAT MY HEART AS THOUGH IT WERE A
    FRAGILE FLOWER
AND THAT SHE'D LAY HER DOWN FOR ME TO LOVE HER HOUR
    ON HOUR

I SAID I'D NOT BE PLAYED UPON LIKE BREATH UPON A SPARK
I WARNED HER OF MY DANGER AND I WARNED HER OF MY
    DARK
AND WHEN THE TIME HAD COME FOR ME TO WEND ME ON
    MY WAY
I SAID SHE'D SEE MY FACE AGAIN UPON A DISTANT DAY

BUT IF I LOVE, A PART OF ME MUST HATE
AND IF I LAUGH, A PART OF ME MUST CRY
OH, IF I STAY, A PART OF ME MUST GO
AND AS I LIVE, A PART OF ME MUST DIE

JOAN LITTLEWOOD It was what I would come to know as
classic Jimmie Miller: lashings of self-pity coupled with
the empathy of a mackerel, /all wrapped up in delicious
poetry and pain.

JOAN 2 /all wrapped up in delicious poetry and pain.

JOAN LITTLEWOOD This was, of course, before he grew a beard
and became a genius.

JIMMIE MILLER	COMPANY
BUT TIME DOES NOT REWARD US FOR NEGLECTING THOSE WHO LOVE	HMM
MY DARLING LIES BENEATH THE EARTH WHILE I REMAIN ABOVE	HMM
AND FOR THE BITTER WORDS AND FOR THE LEAVING THAT I TOOK	HMM
MY PENANCE IS TO LIVE BESIDE THE RAVEN AND THE ROOK	HMM

JIMMIE MILLER and **COMPANY**

FOR IF I LOVE, A PART OF ME MUST HATE
AND IF I LAUGH, A PART OF ME MUST CRY
OH, IF I STAY, A PART OF ME MUST GO
AND AS I LIVE, A PART OF ME MUST DIE

JOAN 2 I'm having some of that.

JIMMIE MILLER That's nice, but I've got to go. A meeting of the Workers' Theatre Group, AKA the Red Megaphones. We might be a little bit Communist. Solidarity. Fuck Hitler. That sort of thing.

JOAN 2 *clicks her heels.*

JOAN 2 Fuck Hitler.

JIMMIE MILLER Meet me there? One hundred-and-eleven A, Grosvenor Street. Nine o'clock.

JIMMIE MILLER *exits.*

JOAN LITTLEWOOD That was also what I'd come to know as classic Jimmie: an invitation, then off like a hare. I was hooked. And of course, later that night, I was there, waiting outside, /nine o'clock on the dot.

Scene Ten

*Outside one hundred-and-eleven A, Grosvenor Street,
Manchester.* JOAN 2 *is hanging around.* JIMMIE MILLER
appears.

JIMMIE MILLER /Nine o'clock on the dot. We're on a break.
Smoke?

JOAN 2 Naturally.

They smoke.

JIMMIE MILLER So listen. You should know that I work from
certain principles one: that the trouble with modernity is
consumption; two: that the trouble with consumption is
waste, and three: that working people don't see theatre as an
art form that has anything to do with them, so they don't go.

JOAN 2 So this is about democratisation of an art form, is it?
What we do with our own unworthy scaffold? *(To* AUDIENCE*)*
That's a quote from Henry V.

JOAN LITTLEWOOD I was on fire.

JOAN 2 *(to* JIMMIE MILLER *)* I once directed this production
of Macbeth...

JIMMIE MILLER You're not supposed to say that.

JOAN 2 Superstition is the opiate of the people.

JIMMIE MILLER I thought that was religion.

JOAN 2 Isn't religion just organised superstition? Anyway: back
to my Macbeth. I was twelve.

JIMMIE MILLER That's precocious.

JOAN 2 Because I'm a woman, or because I'm poor? Or simply
because I had an opinion as a child? I wasn't precocious;
I was under-age.

JIMMIE MILLER Please go on.

JOAN 2 I will. My production had no table, no chairs, just everyone squatting, a tablecloth held taut between them. Took minutes away from clunky scene changes, and kept everyone on their toes.

JIMMIE MILLER And the budget down. So we're also talking about an aesthetic of economy.

JOAN 2 Profligacy is in bad taste.

JIMMIE MILLER Profligacy is the nadir of bad taste. And on a domestic note, economic use of means and of space is essential. Why have two rooms when you can have one? Why have two beds when one will do?

JOAN 2 What you're saying is that it would not only be economical for us to sleep together, but therefore that it would also, intrinsically, be in extremely bad taste for us not to do so. That there is a moral, aesthetic and economical imperative for us to fuck.

JIMMIE MILLER I've never met anyone like you.

HOWARD *appears.*

HOWARD Break's over.

JIMMIE MILLER *(to* **JOAN 2***)* Coming?

HOWARD *(to* **JOAN 2***)* I'm Howard.

Scene Eleven

JOAN LITTLEWOOD One hundred-and-eleven A, Grosvenor Street, Manchester. The Headquarters of the Red Megaphones Theatre Company. How To Ingratiate Yourself Immediately With New Colleagues.

One hundred-and-eleven A, Grosvenor Street, Manchester: a studio space above a warehouse. **HOWARD**, **ROSALIE** *and* **OTHERS** *are sitting in a circle.* **JIMMIE MILLER** *and* **JOAN 2** *join them.*

HOWARD This is Rosalie.

JOAN 2 Pleased to meet you. I'm /Joan.

ROSALIE /Joan. I know. The Stockwell Urchin.

JOAN 2 Word travels.

ROSALIE RADA, wasn't it?

HOWARD *(to* **JIMMIE MILLER** *)* You're kidding.

JIMMIE MILLER What?

HOWARD I'm not having that. Every spare minute we're in here, working our arses off, protesting the impoverishment of the workers, and all the while she's been down south, working on healthy vowel movement.

JIMMIE MILLER Every spare minute, Howard? I've the register /here.

ROSALIE /Don't, /Jimmie.

JIMMIE MILLER /Last Tuesday: late; Wednesday: no show; Sunday: at church, /apparently.

HOWARD /My brother's /wedding!

ROSALIE /Howard! Joan left RADA /early.

HOWARD /We cannot have your prick as our casting director, Jimmie.

JIMMIE MILLER Come here and say that.

> **HOWARD** *steps towards* **JIMMIE MILLER** .

HOWARD We cannot have your prick—

> **JIMMIE MILLER** *raises his fist.* **JOAN 2** *steps between them.*

JOAN 2 Hold it! Step apart.

JIMMIE MILLER What?

JOAN 2 Apart. (**JIMMIE MILLER** *and* **HOWARD** *separate)* Further. (**JIMMIE MILLER** *and* **HOWARD** *move according to* **JOAN 2***'s instructions)* Bit more... That's right. Now carry on.

HOWARD What?

JOAN 2 *(to* **JIMMIE MILLER** *)* You wanted to punch him. So punch him.

JIMMIE MILLER What are you doing?

JOAN 2 New girl arrives; men fight over her: it's a bit derivative, but the dialogue is spicy – I'll give you that. The problem is that you've fallen into the trap of naturalism, which makes it banal. Take it from Howard's line, "we cannot have your prick," – the first one – only this time, instead of getting closer, step further apart.

HOWARD We cannot have your prick as our casting director, Jimmie.

JIMMIE MILLER Come here and say that.

> **HOWARD** *steps further away.* **JIMMIE MILLER** *mirrors him.*

JOAN 2 Good. Line.

HOWARD We cannot have your prick—

Throughout the following speech, **JIMMIE MILLER** , **HOWARD** *and* **ROSALIE** *follow* **JOAN 2**'s *instructions to the letter.*

JOAN 2 Now slow motion! The rest of you: hum. Something low, dramatic, foreboding.

[MUSIC NO. 8A: "CHOPIN FUNERAL MARCH"]

Jimmie: draw your fist back like an arrow on a bow. Howard: you didn't think he meant it. Jimmie: the punch should flow as though through thick molasses. Howard: it's a right hook. Your jaw leads, followed by your eyes then the rest of you... And relax.

ROSALIE *bursts out laughing.* **JIMMIE MILLER** *and* **HOWARD** *join in.* **JOAN 2** *smiles at them.*

Yes? You see, Howard, you're right. About RADA, that is. They taught classes on how to sip fake sherry whilst moving imperceptibly downstage in search of a better sightline. I'm...less of a finishing school, more of a workshop, you might say.

HOWARD They must have hated you.

JOAN 2 The single class we had on what they called 'Politicised Theatre' involved a stark warning against overestimating the intellectual capabilities of the working classes.

ROSALIE And you said...

JOAN 2 'No ballet for the natives, then?'

JIMMIE MILLE A good line.

HOWARD I've never met anyone like you.

JOAN 2 There must be an echo in here.

JOAN LITTLEWOOD *edges towards* **ROSALIE.**

JOAN LITTLEWOOD *(to* **ROSALIE**, *indicating the* **AUDIENCE***)* Rosalie, this is all ravishingly interesting, but I think everyone would like to get to the bit when Gerry appears. Can we crack on?

ROSALIE *(to* **JOAN LITTLEWOOD***)* Couple more scenes.

JOAN LITTLEWOOD Couple more scenes. Right-ho. *(To* **JIMMIE MILLER** , **JOAN 2** *and* **HOWARD***)* Don't mind me.

JOAN LITTLEWOOD *sits down once more.*

JIMMIE MILLER So?

HOWARD *(to* **JOAN 2***)* You're in.

JOAN 2 Super.

ROSALIE In which case it's time for the scene in Jimmie's mum's kitchen, isn't it?

Scene Twelve

Year counter counts to 1935.

JOAN LITTLEWOOD   Scene twelve. The Millers' home: thirty seven, Coburg Street, Salford. How Not To Let History Repeat Itself.

The kitchen of the Miller's home at thirty seven, Coburg street. **JIMMIE** *sits at the table.* **JOAN 2** *vomits into the kitchen sink.* **JOAN 2** *turns to the* **AUDIENCE**.

JOAN 2   Shit.

JOAN 2 steps out of the kitchen. **JIMMIE MILLER** *exits.*

[MUSIC NO. 9: "GOODBYE"]

Music starts, as underscore. **CAROLINE EMILY** *appears, a piece of paper in her hand.*

CAROLINE EMILY   Here's the address. Kate sorted it. The money, I mean.

JOAN 2   Right.

CAROLINE EMILY   I'll come for you, after.

JOAN 2   Right.

CAROLINE EMILY   Joan?

JOAN 2   Yes?

CAROLINE EMILY   It won't be painless.

JOAN 2   I'll not flinch. Hand me the bottle of gin and the knitting needle, and I'll do it myself.

During the following verses, **THE COMPANY** *takes* **JOAN 2** *into the abortionist's house and lays her down on a bed, while she sings.*

JOAN 2

> IT'S GOODBYE
> NOT FOR A WHILE
> BUT FOR FOREVER;
> AND I'LL NEVER SEE YOUR SMILE
> AND WE'LL NOT HATE
> AND WE'LL NOT FIGHT
> AND YOU WILL NEVER CRY YOURSELF TO SLEEP AT NIGHT

JOAN LITTLEWOOD *(to* **JOAN 2***)* I'm going to go and see if I can find Gerry. You carry on, love. You're doing a terrific job. Terrific. I'm fine. I'll be back in a minute. Just need a breath of air. I won't be long. *(to* **AUDIENCE***)* I don't like the way they do this bit.

JOAN LITTLEWOOD *exits.*

JOAN 2

> CHANGE IS NOT AN OPTION IT'S THE

	ENSEMBLE
NATURE	AH
OF LIFE	AH
CHANGE IS NEITHER	AH
PRIVILEGE NOR CURSE	
	AH, AH
STRANGE TO THINK	AH
THAT I COULD JUST BE	
SOMEBODY'S	
MOTHER, SOMEONE'S WIFE	
HELP ME PUT THOSE	MM
WHEELS INTO REVERSE	

> I'D LIKE TO MAKE
> ONE LAST REQUEST
> PLEASE UNDERSTAND
> THAT WHAT I'VE PLANNED IS FOR THE BEST
> THE FACT IS, LIFE
> IS OVERBLOWN
> AND SO YOU'LL NEVER KNOW THE LONELINESS I'VE KNOWN

IT'S GOODBYE
GOODBYE
GOODBYE

As the song ends, **JOAN 3** *takes the cap from* **JOAN 2**.

Scene Thirteen

One hundred-and-eleven A, Grosvenor Street, Manchester.
THE COMPANY, *minus* **JOAN LITTLEWOOD** *and the
actor who plays* **JEAN NEWLOVE**. **JOAN 3** *addresses the*
COMPANY *and the* **AUDIENCE**, *equally. Year counter
counts to 1937.*

JOAN 3 Scene thirteen. We are our own training ground.
Movement. Voice. Audibility. Reliability. Flexibility.

JOAN LITTLEWOOD *enters.*

JOAN LITTLEWOOD And I'm back in the room.

JOAN 3 Well, find a seat and join in.

JOAN LITTLEWOOD Who the fuck are you?

JOAN 3 Joan.

JOAN LITTLEWOOD Self-appointed? That's bold.

JOAN 3 We women make our own luck. And you age, as you
said earlier. Besides, you'd buggered off. Now then: are you
staying?

JOAN LITTLEWOOD Am I staying! Of course I'm bloody well
/staying!

JOAN 3 /Then find a seat.

JOAN LITTLEWOOD *sits down.*

JOAN LITTLEWOOD *(to* **AUDIENCE***)* Am I staying!

JOAN 3 *addresses the* **COMPANY** *plus the* **AUDIENCE**.

JOAN 3 Now then, all of you – yes, all of you; there's no such
thing as an innocent bystander – repeat after me: me, you,
us and them.

ALL Me, you, us and them.

JOAN 3 Clearer.

ALL Me, you, us and them.

JOAN 3 Glide through the consonants.

ALL Me, you, us and them.

JOAN 3 Now lament.

ALL Me, you, us and them.

JOAN 3 It's a secret.

ALL Me, you, us and them.

JOAN 3 It's a joke.

ALL Me, you, us and them.

JOAN 3 It's not funny.

ALL Me, you, us and them.

JOAN 3 *(to* **HOWARD***)* Reverse it.

HOWARD Them and us, you, me.

JOAN 3 Together.

ALL Them and us, you, me.

JOAN 3 Not bad, for beginners. Now for some movement. I came across the work of a brilliant teacher called Rudolph Laban, who—

JEAN NEWLOVE *enters.*

JEAN NEWLOVE I do hope I'm not interrupting.

JOAN 3 It depends. What's your speciality?

JEAN NEWLOVE Movement. Rudolph Laban.

JOAN 3 Your timing is so serendipitous as to be suspicious.

JEAN NEWLOVE I'll need a drum. And a circle. Clear the chairs. Close your eyes. *(To the* **AUDIENCE***)* You, too. All of you. Listen to yourself. How are you being? Where's your breath falling? Where hurts? Where feels good? This is your space. This is the space you inhabit. This is your home. And this is

your language. Your existence. Open your eyes. Hold on to
that sense of space, the space you inhabit, your home. *(To*
JOAN 3*)* I'm Jean. Jean Newlove. I've come about the theatre.

JIMMIE MILLER *steps forward to take* **JEAN NEWLOVE***'s
hand.*

JIMMIE MILLER Jimmie Miller.

JOAN 3 Well, this is already a complete and resolute pleasure,
Jean. I'm Joan. You've met Jimmie.

ROSALIE *(to* **GERRY RAFFLES***, in the* **AUDIENCE***)* You're on!

JIMMIE MILLER *(putting his arm around* **JEAN NEWLOVE***)* So
listen. You should know that I work from certain principles,
one: that the trouble with modernity is consumption...

JIMMIE MILLER *and* **JEAN NEWLOVE** *wander off.* **GERRY
RAFFLES** *climbs eagerly on stage.*

GERRY RAFFLES Hello? I've come about the theatre.

JOAN 3 *turns to* **GERRY RAFFLES**. **JOAN LITTLEWOOD**
walks up, too. **ROSALIE** *and* **HOWARD** *step forward.*
HOWARD *swiftly takes* **GERRY RAFFLES***' hand and
shakes it.*

HOWARD Howard.

GERRY RAFFLES Gerry.

HOWARD Glad you could make it. Come with me.

HOWARD *takes* **GERRY RAFFLES** *off into a corner and
engages him in conversation.* **JOAN 3** *goes to follow them.*
ROSALIE *stops her.*

ROSALIE *(to* **JOAN 3***)* You weren't there. Not when he first
arrived. You're ill in bed. An attack of quinsy, remember?

JOAN 3 Shit. Sorry. Got caught up in it.

ROSALIE It's fine. I may have cued him too soon. Anyway.

JOAN LITTLEWOOD But this is that bit we've all been waiting for. When she—

ROSALIE She – you...it doesn't change the facts.

JOAN LITTLEWOOD I've never let truth get in the way of a good story.

ROSALIE *(to* **JOAN 3***)* You need to go, otherwise the whole night will unravel.

JOAN 3 See you later.

JOAN LITTLEWOOD *(to* **JOAN 3***)* If you hadn't missed your cue to leave, this wouldn't have happened. Fucking amateur.

ROSALIE *(to* **JOAN LITTLEWOOD***)* Now: you're going to go and make yourself a cup of tea; *(to* **JOAN 3***)* I'm going to get things back on track.

> **JOAN 3** *exits*.

JOAN LITTLEWOOD Oh I see: I'm getting in the way of my own life story, am I?

ROSALIE You always do.

> **JOAN LITTLEWOOD** *exits*.

ROSALIE *(to* **AUDIENCE***)* Directors think they're in control: that is their tragedy; actors know they're not: that is theirs. *(To* **GERRY RAFFLES***)* Sorry about that. What was your name?

GERRY RAFFLES Raffles. Gerry Raffles. It's a funny name.

ROSALIE It's a nice name, actually. A bit funny, you're right. I recognise you. From the university, yes?

GERRY RAFFLES Yes.

ROSALIE I'm Rosalie. You've met Howard. What brings you here?

GERRY RAFFLES The need to do something other than sit and study and wonder what the real world is like. The desire to make a difference.

HOWARD How old are you?

GERRY RAFFLES Seventeen in April.

HOWARD Ever performed?

GERRY RAFFLES A little. At school. But I'm good with my hands, too. I can make things. Fix things. Build sets, put up lights. I'm good for it.

ROSALIE Maybe we can be your university. You're very welcome, Gerry, and not only because you're tall. Though that will no doubt come in very handy.

GERRY RAFFLES My dad's in the cloth business. He said he might be able to give us some old stock at cost.

ROSALIE Music to my ears. Howard, would you show Gerry around?

>   **HOWARD** *and* **GERRY RAFFLES** *exit.* **JOAN LITTLEWOOD** *enters, carrying a cup of tea.*

ROSALIE That was quick.

JOAN LITTLEWOOD Well I didn't want to miss anything.

ROSALIE I see.

JOAN LITTLEWOOD Don't ever do that to me again.

ROSALIE I didn't mean to upset you.

JOAN LITTLEWOOD I'm not upset. I could recast you at the drop of a hat. You're not all that, you know.

ROSALIE That's fair.

JOAN LITTLEWOOD Don't patronise me, otherwise I'll be forced to take matters into my own hands.

ROSALIE Your own hands? This whole thing is your own hands, Joan. Everything we're doing.

JOAN LITTLEWOOD He's dead.

ROSALIE He's just arrived. He's sixteen. You're twenty-three. Admittedly, you don't look it right now.

JOAN LITTLEWOOD Fuck you.

ROSALIE We're telling the story of a theatrical revolutionary.

JOAN LITTLEWOOD That's me.

ROSALIE That's you. And, if we tell the story in the right order, you see Gerry again. You go off-piste, and he disappears. He doesn't exist without you.

JOAN LITTLEWOOD Don't exaggerate.

ROSALIE He doesn't even have a Wikipedia page, Joan. Sure, there's a square in Stratford – the other one – named after him *(OR: the square outside is named after him)*, but few could tell you why. You're the only reason anyone gives a fig. About any of us, for that matter. And right now, you're at risk of screwing that up.

JOAN LITTLEWOOD Alright, alright.

ROSALIE So: you're a charismatic theatrical revolutionary.

JOAN LITTLEWOOD I'm a charismatic theatrical revolutionary.

> **ROSALIE** *indicates the year counter, which counts up to 1940.*

ROSALIE It's 1937. Hitler's in power.

JOAN LITTLEWOOD *(clicking her heels)* Fuck Hitler.

ROSALIE Fuck Hitler. Gerry doesn't die until 1975. You've got thirty-odd years to make the most of him.

JOAN LITTLEWOOD 1975, you say?

ROSALIE Yes 1975.

JOAN LITTLEWOOD That does ring a bell.

ROSALIE Good. *(Indicating the year counter:)* Keep your eye on the year counter and you'll be fine.

JOAN LITTLEWOOD I think it's about time for another song.

ROSALIE What a good idea, Joan. Company!

[MUSIC NO. 10: "THE THEATRE WORKSHOP STORY 1: Fuente Ovejuna]

During the song, the screen shows associated headlines, also the image of Picasso's Guernica.

WE STUDY THE HISTORY OF SOCIAL INJUSTICES,
THE THEORIES OF LABAN, AND THE WORK OF STANISLAVSKY
WE RENAME THE COMPANY 'THEATRE UNION':
UNITING COMMUNITIES, REFLECTING REAL LIFE

AND SO WHEN THE CIVIL WAR BREAKS OUT IN SPAIN
WE SHOW, WITH A PASSION UNCONCEALED
HOW RADICALS BEND BUT NEVER YIELD
WHEN ANYONE ASKS, WE WILLINGLY EXPLAIN
THAT WE ARE POLITICALLY LEFT-WING AND STYLISTICALLY
    LEFT-FIELD

Scene Fourteen

JOAN LITTLEWOOD Scene fourteen: How to Turn a Flirtation into Something Actually Useful.

Year counter counts up to 1938. A bus stop. **JOAN 3** *is waiting.* **GERRY RAFFLES** *appears.*

GERRY RAFFLES Where are you going?

JOAN 3 Home. Well, to the Millers', at least.

GERRY RAFFLES Which bus?

JOAN 3 Any.

GERRY RAFFLES Mind if I wait?

JOAN 3 No need.

GERRY RAFFLES I didn't suggest there was.

JOAN 3 Are you deliberately wrecking my choreography?

GERRY RAFFLES Guilty as charged.

JOAN 3 Ha.

GERRY RAFFLES What do you want?

JOAN 3 What?

GERRY RAFFLES Out of life.

JOAN 3 That's a grand old question, Gerry. I want to show people that they're freer than they think. You?

GERRY RAFFLES I'd like a boat.

JOAN 3 A boat?

GERRY RAFFLES Some day, yes.

JOAN 3 I hate boats.

GERRY RAFFLES Oh.

A bus arrives. **JOAN 3** *doesn't get on it. The bus departs.*

Not the right bus?

JOAN 3 Nope. You can go now, if you like.

    GERRY RAFFLES *doesn't move.*

So are you planning on staying with the company?

GERRY RAFFLES I seem to be.

JOAN 3 Right.

GERRY RAFFLES And what do you make of that?

JOAN 3 That you've found your vocation. But if you really want to do something for me, Gerry, find us a permanent home for our theatre, would you? We're tired of touring.

GERRY RAFFLES I'll get on to it.

    GERRY RAFFLES *takes her hand.* **JOAN 3** *looks at their conjoined hands, then back at him. Another bus arrives.*

JOAN 3 I should take this one.

    GERRY RAFFLES *nods. She gets on the bus and resolutely doesn't look back at* **GERRY RAFFLES** *as the bus pulls away.*

JOAN LITTLEWOOD Smooth, isn't he? Charmer. But I must crack on or I'll get into trouble again.

Scene Fifteen

JOAN LITTLEWOOD Scene fifteen. Grosvenor Street, an emergency meeting: How Censorship Can Focus the Mind, or, How Spontaneous Leadership is an Aphrodisiac.

Year Counter counts up to 1939. Grosvenor Street. **HOWARD, ROSALIE, JEAN NEWLOVE, JOAN 3, GERRY RAFFLES. JIMMIE MILLER** *holds up a letter.*

JIMMIE MILLER They're shutting us down.

JEAN NEWLOVE What?

JIMMIE MILLER The Lord Chamberlain: "Cease and desist".

HOWARD Fucking censors.

JEAN NEWLOVE What for?

JOAN 3 Being current.

JIMMIE MILLER Representing living figures on the stage, actually. Plus: carrying a shovel in a suggestive manner.

ROSALIE I knew that was a bad idea.

HOWARD It got a great laugh.

JEAN NEWLOVE They can't, can they?

JOAN 3 It's either that, or a fine we can't afford.

GERRY RAFFLES Clubs are exempt.

HOWARD From what?

GERRY RAFFLES My dad told me.

JIMMIE MILLER "My Dad told me".

JOAN 3 Jimmie.

GERRY RAFFLES Clubs, you know, like gentlemen's clubs: they can put on whatever they like. The Lord Chamberlain doesn't care. Cabaret, strippers—

JEAN NEWLOVE I'm not stripping.

JIMMIE MILLER *(to* **JEAN***)* No, you're not.

GERRY RAFFLES I'm not suggesting anyone strips. It's something to do with accountability. Clubs are a loophole. Don't ask me why. So what if, instead of tickets, we sell subscriptions?

ROSALIE Like a speakeasy.

GERRY RAFFLES The thrill of prohibition, but totally within the law.

JOAN 3 We can be as current as we like?

GERRY RAFFLES The world's your oyster.

JIMMIE MILLER Censorship is the scythe of a totalitarian regime.

GERRY RAFFLES Nice one, Jimmie.

HOWARD We should start with a proper shocker.

JOAN 3 The Munich Agreement.

GERRY RAFFLES I'll go and get us a licence.

    GERRY RAFFLES *exits. A drum roll.*

JOAN 3 Near a country called Czechoslovakia.

JIMMIE MILLER Whose people are known as the Czechs.

JOAN 3 A fascist called Hitler.

TEDDY (Like Franco, but littler)

JOAN 3 Is growling and flexing his pecs.

TEDDY "I want some more land",*

JOAN 3   declares Hitler.

TEDDY "I don't feel I've had my fair share"

JIMMIE MILLER
    He makes this admission

---

* This should take a German accent.

Of reckless ambition

whilst raising one arm in the air

ALF His neighbour, Signor Mussolini.

GERARD (Who's wearing a shirt that is black)

TEDDY Says:

JEAN NEWLOVE

"give him a chance-A[**]

he's not asked for france-A

I second his plan of attack"

[MUSIC NO. 11: "THE THEATRE WORKSHOP STORY 2: Last Edition] begins as an undersore.

JOAN 3 Prime Minister Chamberlain argues:

ROSALIE

"I know it's hard on the czechs[***]

but bribe the dictator

we'll deal with him later

let's offer him prague and relax"

** This should take an Italian accent.
*** This should be Advanced R.P. in which "Czechs" rhymes with "relax"

[MUSIC NO. 11: "THE THEATRE WORKSHOP STORY 2: Last Edition] continued

THE PUNTERS DECLARE OUR SATIRE IS THE BEST
THOUGH SOME ARE INITIALLY APPREHENSIVE
OTHERS INCLINED TO TAKE OFFENCE
BUT EVEN OUR HARSHEST CRITICS ARE IMPRESSED
BECAUSE WE ARE ALWAYS OFF THE WALL AND WE ARE NEVER
    ON THE FENCE

Scene Sixteen

JOAN LITTLEWOOD Scene sixteen: It's 1943 already. I know: history runs at the speed of light. How to Make the Most of a Man in Uniform.

Year counter counts up to 1943. Stratford-Upon-Avon. The noise of a train. **JOAN 3** *enters and looks about her, expectantly.* **GERRY RAFFLES***, wearing an RAF uniform and carrying a bunch of parma violets, runs on. He picks* **JOAN 3** *up and swings her round. They laugh.*

GERRY RAFFLES Business or pleasure?

JOAN 3 As an artist, I've never had the luxury of making that distinction. You look sexy in that.

GERRY RAFFLES You look sexy in everything.

JOAN 3 Ha, ha. Is that the Festival theatre?

GERRY RAFFLES It is. I've tickets.

JOAN 3 Must we?

GERRY RAFFLES Think of it as research.

Sounds of **AUDIENCE** *chattering.* **GERRY RAFFLES** *and* **JOAN 3** *take their seats.* **JOAN LITTLEWOOD** *appears wearing an* **USHERETTE***'s hat. Audio of a period recording from Julius Caesar.*

JOAN 3 The Cobbler sounds just like Caesar. They think we're idiots.

JOAN LITTLEWOOD Sh!

GERRY RAFFLES Well, the lighting's just as I'd hoped.

JOAN 3 Do they know we're at war? Mussolini's just crumpled. It's set in Rome, for fuck's sake.

JOAN LITTLEWOOD Please.

JOAN 3 And togas: really? Stick them in black shirts, even this audience would erupt.

JOAN LITTLEWOOD I'm going to have to ask you to leave.

JOAN 3 I'm going to have to take you up on that offer. *(to* **GERRY***)* She's the best thing in it.

Sound of applause. **JOAN LITTLEWOOD** *removes her* **USHERETTE***'s hat.*

It's late. I'm tired. I've still to find a hotel.

GERRY RAFFLES I found us one.

JOAN 3 Right.

GERRY RAFFLES They'd only one room. I booked it in your name. Mr Littlewood at your service.

JOAN 3 I suppose there's nothing for it, then. You'll/sleep on the floor.

GERRY RAFFLES /sleep on the floor. Yes.

JOAN 3 It's heaven, being here, with you.

They kiss. Lights fade on **GERRY RAFFLES** *and* **JOAN 3**. *A spotlight reveals* **JOAN LITTLEWOOD**.

JOAN LITTLEWOOD Our first night together. Maestro?

Music starts.

[MUSIC NO. 12: "NOW"]

NOW IS THE ONLY THING THAT'S REAL
NOW IS THE ONE THING THAT WE REALLY FEEL
THE SPARK OF INVENTION
THE BONE OF CONTENTION
THE THRILL OF SEDUCTION...
NOW IS THE ONLY TIME TO CARE
NOW IS THE ONE THING THAT IS REALLY THERE
THE PAST LIES IN TATTERS; THE FUTURE?
WELL, ANYHOW,

NOTHING ELSE MATTERS, BUT NOW

Underscore continues. Lights up on a hotel room. **GERRY RAFFLES** *and* **JOAN 3** *are in bed, asleep.* **JOAN 3** *wakes up, suddenly.*

JOAN 3 Gerry!

GERRY RAFFLES What is it?

JOAN 3 There was an air raid. The theatre was on fire. I couldn't rescue you.

GERRY RAFFLES A nightmare. I'm safe. Sleep.

JOAN 3 Sing to me.

GERRY RAFFLES
SOME FOLK SIGN ON A DOTTED LINE
OTHERS WISH UPON A STAR
I WON'T HAVE A BAR OF THAT GUFF
YOU, AND WE ARE ENOUGH FOR ME

Lullabied by **GERRY RAFFLES**, **JOAN 3** *falls asleep again. Lights up on* **JOAN LITTLEWOOD** *once more, and she and* **GERRY RAFFLES** *sing together. During the final section of the song,* **GERRY RAFFLES** *gets up, and gets dressed once more.*

JOAN LITTLEWOOD and **GERRY RAFFLES** *(staggered)*
NOW IS THE ONLY THING SET FAST
NOW IS THE ONE THING THAT WILL REALLY LAST
THE SIMPLEST OF PLEASURES
THE RICHEST OF TREASURES
THE THRILL OF SEDUCTION...

NOW IS THE ONLY THING THAT'S HERE
NOW IS THE ONLY THING THAT'S REALLY SINCERE
THE PAST LIES IN TATTERS; THE FUTURE?
WELL, ANYHOW,
NOTHING ELSE MATTERS, BUT...

GERRY RAFFLES *kisses* **JOAN 3** *and exits, leaving* **JOAN LITTLEWOOD** *to sing the final word on her own.*

...NOW.

Scene Seventeen

*Year counter counts up to 1945. There is a massive noise
of an explosion, and the screen shows Hiroshima.*

JOAN LITTLEWOOD And now: Hiroshima, or: The Making
of Uranium 235, or: How a Piece of Political Propaganda
Doesn't Half Focus the Creative Mind.

HOWARD *enters with a large sheaf of papers.*

JOAN 3 I say, I say, I say: what have you got there?

HOWARD The Smyth report on Hiroshima. *(Reads)* "A General
Account of the Development of Methods of Using Atomic
Energy for Military Purposes."

JOAN 3 Blimey, that sounds interesting!

HOWARD It is. And apparently the only science they've
missed out is the stuff a tiny little mind like mine wouldn't
understand.

JOAN 3 Any mention of the chronic toxicity of radioactive decay?

HOARD No.

JOAN 3 The tens of thousands of civilian deaths?

HOWARD No.

JOAN 3 How nuclear warfare signifies the height of scientific
knowledge and the end of humanity?

HOWARD No.

JOAN 3 Right. Jimmie?

Enter **JIMMIE MILLER.**

JIMMIE MILLER I've changed my name to Ewan. Ewan MacColl.

HOWARD Draft-dodger.

JIMMIE MILLER It's about my ethnicity.

JOAN 3 I don't give a shit what it's about, and I don't mind which one of you does it, Jimmie – you or Ewan – but I'd like at least one of you to write me a play.

JIMMIE MILLER About what?

JOAN 3 About how – three days after the single most devastating act of man's inhumanity against man – they've essentially published a fucking advert.

> **JOAN 3** *hands* **JIMMIE MILLER** *the Smyth report.*

JIMMIE MILLER I'll get going.

> **PEARL TURNER** *enters, wearing a smart red coat.* **JIMMIE MILLER** *looks her up and down, then exits.*

PEARL TURNER Miss Littlewood? I'm Pearl Turner. From Chichester. I've come about the theatre.

JOAN 3 Can you sing?

PEARL TURNER It's what I do.

JOAN LITTLEWOOD Excellent.

JOAN 3 *(To* **PEARL TURNER** *)* You're in. That coat, though. Give it here. Far too bourgeois for our company, darling. *(***JOAN 3** *takes the coat from* **PEARL TURNER** *)* You look like you've been dressed by your mother. Now then, Howard, would you show Pearly Bird around?

> **HOWARD** *exits with* **PEARL TURNER** .

ROSALIE Joan?

JOAN 3 Yes, Rosalie?

ROSALIE Meeting with the Arts Council.

JOAN 3 Right you are.

> **JOAN 3** *puts on* **PEARL TURNER**'s *coat.* **ROSALIE** *raises her eyebrows.*

Don't look at me in that tone of voice, Rosalie. Nothing's too bourgeois for the Arts Council. It's a costume. Or a weapon. You choose. Besides, the colour did nothing for Pearl's complexion.

JOAN LITTLEWOOD *enters as the* **ARTS COUNCIL.**

JOAN LITTLEWOOD   How To Woo The Arts Council! *(To* **AUDIENCE***)* I'm the Arts Council. I love this bit: I get to play a wanker.

JOAN 3 I can't work like this any more.

JOAN LITTLEWOOD No problem. *(To wings)* Next!

JOAN 4 *appears.*

Hello, Cuckoo. Ready to take over?

JOAN 4 Yes.

JOAN LITTLEWOOD Good.

JOAN 3 What?

JOAN LITTLEWOOD I age.

JOAN 3 Now?

JOAN LITTLEWOOD You're an interloper. You had a decent innings. And you called my bluff. Now hand over the cap and move on, would you? I've got a scene to play.

JOAN 3 Shit.

JOAN 4 You've literally only got yourself to blame.

JOAN 3 You've literally got to watch your back from now on.

JOAN 3 *hands over the cap to* **JOAN 4***, and exits.* **JOAN 3** *takes* **PEARL TURNER***'s coat off and gives it to* **JOAN 4***, who puts it on.*

JOAN LITTLEWOOD *(to* **AUDIENCE***)* I like to garner a spirit of healthy competition amongst my actors. *(To* **JOAN4***)* Right, love. Know where we are? Jimmie's writing/ the Hiroshima play—

JOAN 4 /The Hiroshima play. Yes, you're the Arts Council, I'm asking for money.

JOAN LITTLEWOOD Blimey. Take it from: "So you see, our latest /play..."

JOAN 4 So you see, our latest play – yet to be premiered—

JOAN LITTLEWOOD Good girl.

JOAN 4 —is addressing the very most up to date issues, historically, politically and sociologically, fusing cutting edge dramatic practice with popular forms of entertainment to edify and educate. In addition, we'll be touring to places and audiences with very little access to theatre, with an unbelievably broad age range.

ROSALIE We open in a tent. In Filey. Butlins.

JOAN LITTLEWOOD First of all, thank you for the time and trouble you've taken to be here. Secondly, this sounds like a terrific project. There are a couple of points on which your application falls down. We are in the habit of supporting companies who have a base for their work.

JOAN 4 But that's our point: to take theatre to places where there is none at present.

JOAN LITTLEWOOD Such endeavours entertain a level of financial risk to which we at the Arts Council are ethically averse, and so it is with great regret that I must tell you we are unable to offer any financial help at this point in time.

ROSALIE You finance the opera. Operas cost eighty percent more than they take at the box office. And the ballet, and the West End? You're helping them, but not us?

JOAN LITTLEWOOD Unfortunately I can't go into details on other applications. However, you may be pleased to know that this rejection in no way precludes you from applying at a future date. Good day.

JOAN LITTLEWOOD *exits.*

JOAN 4 They sit at their tidy desks with their pencil sharpeners and their sick pay and they look down on us who have more guts in our little fingers than they'll find in their entire lives.

ROSALIE What'll we do now?

JOAN 4 Economise. You could eat less, for a start.

> **ROSALIE** *exits.* **GERRY RAFFLES** *appears in civvies.*

You bastard! Not a word for months. You bastard!

GERRY RAFFLES I was in solitary until they decided to kick me out, once and for all.

JOAN 4 For what?

GERRY RAFFLES Aversion to discipline.

JOAN 4 I'll give you discipline. Now: where's Jimmie?

> **JIMMIE MILLER** *enters holding a script aloft.*

JIMMIE MILLER *(holding up script)* Finished!

JOAN 4 Title?

JIMMIE MILLER Uranium 235. It's the/ weapons grade uranium used in the Little Boy bomb—

JOAN 4 /Weapons grade uranium used in the Little Boy bomb that was dropped on Hiroshima, yes: I know. We haven't got a set. Howard?

> **HOWARD** *enters.*

How much is in the kitty?

HOWARD Five pounds.

JOAN LITTLEWOOD *(to* **AUDIENCE***)* In today's money, ladies and gentlemen, that's...five pounds.

JOAN 4 More than enough for a set.

GERRY RAFFLES While you're busying yourselves with that, I'll go find us a permanent home.

JOAN 4 One less mouth to feed.

GERRY RAFFLES *exits*.

Scene Eighteen

Year counter counts up to 1946.

JOAN LITTLEWOOD   How To Make Your Point Politically, Sociologically and Theatrically, Albeit in the Absence of a Square Meal.

[MUSIC NO. 13: "THE THEATRE WORKSHOP STORY 3 (Reprise: Uranium 235)"]

COMPANY
WE LEARN ABOUT MOLECULES, ATOMS AND NUCLEONS
THEN MAKE UP A DANCE WE CALL THE SUB-ATOMIC BALLET
WE STUDY DEMOCRITUS, BRUNO AND TREVISAN
WE TALK ABOUT ALCHEMY, AND ARROGANCE, AND DEATH

WE OPEN OUR SHOW AT BUTLINS, BY THE SEA
THE HOLIDAYMAKERS GO BERSERK
IN TRUE VINDICATION OF OUR WORK
FOR THEY'RE NOT YOUR USUAL THEATRE BOURGEOISIE
WHICH ONLY REDOUBLES OUR RESENTMENT OF THAT SMUG
    ARTS COUNCIL BERK

COMPANY *exits, leaving* **JOAN 4** *alone.* **PEARL TURNER** *enters.*

PEARL TURNER   Joan? Can I have a word?

JOAN 4   What is it, Pearl?

PEARL TURNER   I don't really know how to say it. I've, I'm, well, the short and the long of it is, I'm pregnant.

JOAN 4   Mmm.

PEARL TURNER   And so I'm going to have to leave.

JOAN 4   Mmm.

PEARL TURNER   And I'm sad about it, but there it is.

JOAN 4   Mmm.

PEARL TURNER Well say something.

JOAN 4 Mmm.

PEARL TURNER Anything.

> **JOAN LITTLEWOOD** *enters and surreptitiously hands*
> **JOAN 4 PEARL TURNER**'s *coat.*

JOAN 4 Is it about the coat? Tell me it's not about the coat.

PEARL TURNER It's not about the coat, Joan.

JOAN 4 You'll move in with Gerry and me. We've got an entire company ready and willing to form the greatest crèche ever known to man, beast or actor. What better education for a child than our willing and erudite company? And what greater love than that of our full-hearted merry band?

PEARL TURNER I'm afraid that's not what I want.

JOAN 4 Oh...oh, I see. Well I have some experience in the other option. How far gone are you?

PEARL TURNER Oh for God's sake, Joan. There is a world beyond your theatre. I love you and I love the company, but I am leaving to live with my husband and to raise our child.

> **JOAN 4** *drops to her knees.*

JOAN 4 You're breaking my heart, Pearl. I can't live without you. I've never known anyone like you and I'll never love again. I'm begging you: don't leave me. Please, don't leave me.

> **PEARL TURNER** *kneels down and takes* **JOAN 4** *in her arms.*

PEARL TURNER Now then, dearest, crazy Joan. I'd always wondered what kind of an actress you were. Now I know. I'm leaving at the end of the season. And for the rest of my life I will be watching you with admiration and adoration with a proud tear in my eye.

JOAN 4 I wonder, when we're sixty, which one of us will be able to say that we've been happy?

> **PEARL TURNER** *kisses* **JOAN 4** *on the forehead, then leaves.* **HOWARD** *walks in, followed at a distance by* **JOHN BURY**.

HOWARD Everything alright, Joan?

JOAN 4 Absolutely, Howard. Just having a chat with Pearl about the sub-atomic ballet sequence. She feels – and I agree – that you've all been rather wimpish about manhandling her, recently, and it's lacking the dynamism we found in our early rehearsals. You really need to throw her around, otherwise it's just not nuclear enough. She's more robust than she might appear. Can you sort that out?

HOWARD Yes. I'll talk to the others.

JOAN 4 For tonight.

HOWARD Yes. And Joan?

JOAN 4 Mmm?

> **HOWARD** *introduces* **JOHN BURY**.

HOWARD Chap called John Bury. Calls himself a designer.

JOHN BURY I've come about the theatre.

JOAN 4 Appetite?

JOHN BURY Russian Constructivism, mainly. Alexandra Exeter—

JOAN 4 No, how much do you eat?

JOHN BURY My nickname's Camel.

JOAN 4 Sounds promising.

HOWARD Oh, and Joan?

JOAN 4 Yes?

HOWARD Nothing to be concerned about, but after the show tonight, we'll be heading off.

JOAN 4 Who?

HOWARD All of us. They're kicking us out of our digs.

JOAN 4 Why?

HOWARD Some idiot gave them the impression we were going to pay rent.

JOAN 4 What'll we do?

HOWARD A quick getaway. I'll put your case in the back of the van.

HOWARD *exits. A telephone rings.* **JOAN 4** *answers the phone.*

JOAN 4 What now?

GERRY RAFFLES *appears holding a telephone receiver.*

GERRY RAFFLES Beloved.

JOAN 4 Where the fuck are you?

GERRY RAFFLES I was in Liverpool. There was a theatre, perfect for us, but...no longer. I'm now in Glasgow. There was a theatre, perfect for us, but—

JOAN 4 Shit.

GERRY RAFFLES Are you eating?

JOAN 4 The Arts Council shafted us.

GERRY RAFFLES Keep your strength up. Howard's got your money.

JOAN 4 Ha. Pearl's leaving. When will you be back?

GERRY RAFFLES Any minute now. I'm losing you. I'll find us a theatre. I'll write. I love you.

JOAN 4 Gerry?

The phone goes dead. **GERRY RAFFLES** *exits.*

JOAN LITTLEWOOD Gerry? I remember every single time I said goodbye. Except the last.

ROSALIE *enters.*

Alright, alright. I get it. I'm out of date. I'll behave.

ROSALIE *exits. Year counter counts up to 1948.*

We set our scene in Middlesborough. Ormesby Hall. Gerry's back with us at last, having failed to find a permanent home. It's 1948. And now: He Fucks Everything Up While I Take It All A Bit Too Seriously.

GERRY RAFFLES *enters followed by* **BARBARA YOUNG**, *who is wearing a beautiful white coat.*

GERRY RAFFLES Joan, can I introduce you to—

BARBARA YOUNG Barbara. Barbara Young. I've come about the theatre.

JOAN 4 That coat: far too bourgeois. Looks like you've been dressed by your mother. Give it here.

BARBARA YOUNG *unwillingly gives her coat to* **JOAN 4**.

(to **BARBARA YOUNG***)* Welcome.

JIMMIE MILLER *enters, carrying a script.*

(to **BARBARA YOUNG** *and* **GERRY RAFFLES***)* Gerry'll show you where the dormitory is, Barbara – won't you, Gerry?

GERRY RAFFLES *exits with* **BARBARA YOUNG**.

Jimmie.

JIMMIE MILLER Ewan.

JOAN 4 Right.

JIMMIE MILLER Script.

JOAN 4 Yes.

JOAN 4 *takes the script from* JIMMIE MILLER *, who exits. A telephone rings.* JOAN 4 *answers it.* JOAN LITTLEWOOD *appears as the* ARTS COUNCIL, *a telephone receiver in her hand.*

JOAN LITTLEWOOD Thank you for your time and trouble. We are in the habit of supporting companies who have a base. Endeavours such as yours entertain a level of financial risk to which we are ethically averse, but this rejection in no way precludes you from reapplying.

JOAN LITTLEWOOD *hangs up.*

JOAN 4 Fuck.

JOAN 4 *lights a cigarette.*

Scene Nineteen

Evening. A bedroom with a gas fire. **JOAN 4** *is reading a script, alone. She turns on a radio.*

[MUSIC NO. 13A: "JOAN ALL ALONE" (Doo-woop reprise plays)]

SONG: "JOAN ALL ALONE" – *Doo-woop reprise* (**ENSEMBLE** *scats underneath*)

ENSEMBLE
SHE'S JOAN
JOAN ALL ALONE FROM HER HEAD TO HER TOES
IF NOBODY LOVES HER, WHAT DOES SHE CARE?
AS JOAN
JOAN ALL ALONE FROM HER HEELS TO HER NOSE
SHE SINGS TO HERSELF, AND PLAYS SOLITAIRE

During the song we first hear and then we see **GERRY RAFFLES** *and* **BARBARA YOUNG** *whispering and laughing, furtively.* **JOAN 4** *watches, unseen by them.* **GERRY RAFFLES** *and* **BARBARA YOUNG** *flirt momentarily, then take hands and run off together, giggling. "JOAN ALL ALONE" – Doo-woop reprise segues directly into* **SONG: "GOODBYE"** *– Reprise.* **JOAN LITTLEWOOD** *enters, helps* **JOAN 4** *into bed and tucks her in.* **JOAN LITTLEWOOD** *might brush* **JOAN 4**'s *hair, stroke her face, give her a book to read – bedtime activities, as gentle and tender as possible – and the song should have the feel of a lullaby.* **JOAN 1**, **JOAN 2** *and* **JOAN 3** *enter as they sing.*

[MUSIC NO. 14: "GOODBYE" (Reprise)]

JOAN LITTLEWOOD
THOUGH IT'S GOODBYE
NOT FOR A WHILE
BUT FOR FOREVER
THOUGH HE'LL NEVER SEE YOU SMILE

YOU'LL NOT PROTECT

JOAN 1, JOAN 2 and **JOAN 3**
OOH...

JOAN LITTLEWOOD
OR, WORSE, PRETEND

JOAN 1, JOAN 2 and **JOAN 3**
OOH...

JOAN LITTLEWOOD
OR WISH ANOTHER DAY WOULD HURRY UP, AND END

JOAN 1, JOAN 2 and **JOAN 3**
DO...

JOAN LITTLEWOOD
CHANGE IS NOT AN OPTION; IT'S THE NATURE OF LOVE/

JOAN 3
NOW IS THE ONLY THING TO BEAR
THE SPARK OF INVENTION/

JOAN 1
I'M JOAN, JOAN ALL ALONE FROM MY HEAD TO MY TOES/

JOAN 2
MY OLD MAN IS SAD HE HAD TO LEAVE ME BEHIND/

JOAN LITTLEWOOD
CHANGE IS NEITHER PRIVILEGE NOR CURSE/

JOAN 1
IF NOBODY LOVES ME, WHAT DO I CARE?/

JOAN 3
THE BONE OF CONTENTION/

JOAN 2
HE'LL SAY "JOAN, YOU'VE NOTHING TO HIDE"/

JOAN 1
JOAN ALL ALONE, ALL ALONE FROM MY HEAD TO MY TOES/

JOAN 2

MY OLD MAN IS ALIVE!/

JOAN 3

THE PAST LIES IN TATTERS/

JOAN LITTLEWOOD

STRANGE THAT SOMETIMES CHANGE ITSELF REQUIRES A
    NUDGE...

JOAN 1

BUT IF, SOMEDAY, SOMEONE SHOULD APPEAR/

JOAN 2

AND ONE DAY, SOME DAY, MY OLD MAN WILL ARRIVE

JOAN 1, JOAN 2 and **JOAN 3**

JOAN ALL ALONE!

JOAN LITTLEWOOD

OR A SHOVE...

JOAN 1, JOAN 2 and **JOAN 3**

JOAN ALL ALONE!

JOAN LITTLEWOOD

GO, BEFORE HE MAKES THE WHOLE THING WORSE

During the following lines, **JOAN 4** *switches on the gas
fire in the room but doesn't light it. The sound of gas.
She sniffs the air.*

I'D LIKE TO MAKE

JOAN 1, JOAN 2 and **JOAN 3**

I'D LIKE TO MAKE:

JOAN LITTLEWOOD

ONE LAST REQUEST

JOAN 1, JOAN 2 and **JOAN 3**

ONE LAST REQUEST

JOAN LITTLEWOOD

PLEASE UNDERSTAND THAT WHAT I'VE PLANNED IS FOR THE
    BEST

JOAN 1, JOAN 2 and **JOAN 3**
ALL FOR THE BEST

JOAN LITTLEWOOD
THE FACT IS, LIFE

JOAN 1, JOAN 2 and **JOAN 3**
AH, LIFE!

JOAN LITTLEWOOD
IS OVERBLOWN/

JOAN 1, JOAN 2 and**JOAN 3**
TOO TRUE!

JOAN LITTLEWOOD
AND SO YOU'LL NEVER KNOW THE LONELINESS I'VE KNOWN
IT'S GOODBYE
GOODBYE
GOODBYE

JOAN LITTLEWOOD *goes to exit. She turns at the last minute.*

(to **AUDIENCE***)* Oblivion. Come back after the interval, to see if there's anything left to see.

JOAN LITTLEWOOD *exits as the lights fade, and the sound of gas rises like a scream.*

Interval

ACT TWO

Scene Twenty

Music: The BAND *begins playing* **"THE NATIONAL ANTHEM"**. *Year counter shows 1953. Enter* JOAN LITTLEWOOD.

JOAN LITTLEWOOD Stop. Stop!

The music comes to a halt.

I'm not having that imperialist crap destroying the tone. Something more stylish, if you please, maestro.

[MUSIC NO. 15: "IN STRATFORD EAST"]

Music starts (vamp).

That's better. *(To* AUDIENCE*)* Welcome back. Now listen: I've got a confession to make. That room, the one we were in before the interval, was so big it would've taken a week and a half to fill with gas. But, like I said, I've never let the truth get in the way of a good story. *(To wings)* You can come back, now!

JOAN 4 *enters.*

Feeling better?

JOAN 4 Much. *(To* AUDIENCE*)* A salient point you missed whilst you were out cavorting in the bar: Jean and Jimmie had a baby, called him Hamish, and asked me to be godmother. I said I wouldn't be good at the god bit; they said I'd be great at the other bits, so we had a deal.

JOAN LITTLEWOOD But the big news...

JOAN 4 But the big news is that – well where is he? Gerry!

GERRY RAFFLES *enters.*

This is your bit. Gerry here atoned for his imperfections by finally following through on his promise to find us a / permanent home.

GERRY RAFFLES /Permanent home. In Stratford.

JOAN 4 Not this one; the other one. *(Or this one!)* London.

GERRY RAFFLES East Fifteen.

JOAN 4 It's 1953. /Welcome.

GERRY RAFFLES /Welcome.

JOAN 4 and **GERRY RAFFLES**

IN STRATFORD EAST
WE ERADICATE ANXIETIES
IN OUR PALACE OF VARIETIES
IN STRATFORD EAST

IN STRATFORD EAST
YOU CAN SING AND LAUGH AND CRY AT EASE
IN OUR PALACE OF VARIETIES
IN STRATFORD EAST

WHEN YOU ARRIVE
YOU'LL BE GREETED AS A FRIEND

JOAN LITTLEWOOD *(spoken)* You might be the only person they speak to, that day

JOAN 4 and **GERRY RAFFLES**

AND WHEN YOU LEAVE
WE'LL LAMENT OUR TIME HAS COME TO AN END
IN STRATFORD EAST
WE'RE THE FRIENDLIEST OF SOCIETIES
IN OUR PALACE OF VARIETIES
IN STRATFORD EAST

JOAN LITTLEWOOD Black Squad!

COMPANY *enters, and sings.*

CHORUS

WE SLAUGHTERED THE RATS

EVICTED THE CATS

THEN CLEANED UP WITH VATS

OF DISINFECTANT

WE STABILISE BEAMS

TO REALISE DREAMS

AND NOW THE WHOLE PLACE SEEMS TO GLOW (AND WE'RE
ALL SO EXPECTANT)

THOUGH SLOW AT FIRST TO FILL, THE HOUSE SELLS OUT
WITHIN THE WEEK

OUR OP'NING SHOW? SHAKESPEARE'S TWELFTH NIGHT

HOWARD

WITH ANDREW AGUECHEEK!

CHORUS

WE'LL GIVE YOU MUCH MORE

THAN GEORGE BERNARD SHAW

WHEN YOU TAKE A TOUR TO STRATFORD EAST!

MM

AVIS BUNNAGE *enters and looks around.*

AVIS BUNNAGE**** Well that's a bloody stupid place to put a stage. Good evening, ladies and gentlemen, my name is Avis Bunnage, and guess what? I've come about the theatre. (*To* **JOAN 4**) Joan, word has it that your actors can speak in their own accent, even if they're Northern.

JOAN 4 Especially if they're Northern.

AVIS BUNNAGE Even in Shakespeare.

*****Avis overcorrects to RP; she shifts not only /u/ as in 'cup' ('buck', 'come', 'shrug', 'Bunnage' etc) to the RP realisation [ʌ], but also all words featuring /u/ as in 'butchers' [ʊ]. I.e. words such as 'sugar', 'nook', 'bullshit' would also take the RP 'cup' vowel sound [ʌ].*

JOAN 4 Especially in Shakespeare.

AVIS BUNNAGE I'm in.

JOAN 4 I'm glad.

AVIS BUNNAGE And I've brought a song about it.

JOAN 4 Please.

AVIS BUNNAGE

MY NAME IS AVIS BUNNAGE
AND THOUGH I'M NORTHERN
DON'T ASSUME I'M COMMON, 'CAUSE I'M NOT.

(spoken) I'm posh Northern.

(sung) IN CHORLTON-CUM-HARDY, WE BUCK THE TREND IN
  NORTHERN VOWELS
FANCY A SAMPLE?
HERE'S AN EXAMPLE, OR TWO:

WE DON'T SAY "BUTCHER'S"*****, WE SAY "BUTCHER'S******;
  BUTCHER'S": THAT'S RIGHT!
WE DON'T SAY "SUGAR"******* WE SAY SUGAR********:

(spoken) Pop to the grocer's and get us a bag of sugar, would
you?

(sung) NOW LISTEN, CAREFULLY, SUGAR
DON'T SHRUG AT PEOPLE SUCH AS ME;
COME TAKE A BUTCHER'S AT STRATFORD EAST!

(spoken) Now shall we try and put those three melodies
together? What do you say, ladies and gentlemen? I can't
hear you! Let's take this baby home!

Year counter counts up to 1954.

***** *Pronounced as per R.P.*
****** *Pronounced as per /u/ in R.P. pronunciation of 'cup'.*
*Avis Bunnage pronounces every /u/ or /oo/ vowel in this way
throughout her performance, except when demonstrating
otherwise.*
******* *Pronounced as per R.P.*
******** *Pronounced as per /u/ in R.P. pronunciation of 'cup'.*

JOAN LITTLEWOOD, JOAN 4, CHORUS *and* **AVIS BUNNAGE**
*sing their respective parts all together, overlapping with
each other–.*

JOAN 4 and **GERRY RAFFLES**

IN STRATFORD EAST
WE ERADICATE ANXIETIES
IN OUR PALACE OF VARIETIES
IN STRATFORD EAST

IN STRATFORD EAST
YOU CAN SING AND LAUGH AND CRY AT EASE
IN OUR PALACE OF VARIETIES
IN STRATFORD EAST

WHEN YOU ARRIVE
YOU'LL BE GREETED AS A FRIEND

JOAN LITTLEWOOD *(spoken)* You might be the only person
they speak to, that day.

JOAN 4 and **GERRY RAFFLES**

AND WHEN YOU LEAVE
WE'LL LAMENT OUR TIME HAS COME TO AN END
IN STRATFORD EAST
WE'RE THE FRIENDLIEST OF SOCIETIES
IN OUR PALACE OF VARIETIES
IN STRATFORD

CHORUS

WE SLAUGHTERED THE RATS
EVICTED THE CATS
THEN CLEANED UP WITH VATS
OF DISINFECTANT
WE STABILISED BEAMS
TO REALISE DREAMS
AND NOW THE PLACE SEEMS TO GLOW (AND WE'RE ALL SO
    EXPECTANT)
THOUGH SLOW AT FIRST TO FILL, THE HOUSE SELLS OUT
    WITHIN THE WEEK

OUR OPENING SHOW? SHAKESPEARE'S TWELFTH NIGHT,
    WITH ANDREW AGUECHEEK
WE'LL GIVE YOU MUCH MORE
THAN GEORGE BERNARD SHAW
WHEN YOU TAKE A TOUR TO STRATFORD

AVIS BUNNAGE

MY NAME IS AVIS BUNNAGE
AND THOUGH I'M NORTHERN
DON'T ASSUME I'M COMMON, 'CAUSE I'M NOT.

(spoken) I'm posh Northern.

(sung) IN CHORLTON-CUM-HARDY, WE BUCK THE TREND IN
    NORTHERN VOWELS
FANCY A SAMPLE? HERE'S AN EXAMPLE, OR TWO:
WE DON'T SAY "BUTCHER'S", WE SAY "BUTCHER'S; BUTCHER'S":
    THAT'S RIGHT!
WE DON'T SAY "SUGAR" WE SAY SUGAR:

(spoken) Pop to the grocer's and get us a bag of sugar, would
you?

(sung) NOW LISTEN, CAREFULLY, SUGAR
DON'T SHRUG AT PEOPLE SUCH AS ME;
COME AND TAKE A BUTCHER'S AT STRATFORD

(spoken:) Some people think the North-South divide is about
class. Personally, I think that's a load of bullshit.********

JOAN LITTLEWOOD, JOAN 4, GERRY RAFFLES and **ENSEMBLE**
IN STRATFORD EAST!

ENSEMBLE

WE'LL GIVE YOU MUCH MORE, IN STRATFORD
THAN GEORGE BERNARD SHAW, IN STRATFORD
WHEN YOU TAKE A TOUR TO STRATFORD EAST!

AVIS BUNNAGE

COME TAKE A BUTCHER'S AT STRATFORD EAST!

******** See earlier footnote on Avis's pronunciation.

*Year counter counts up to 1955. As the song ends, all
exit except for* **JOAN 4**. **HOWARD** *enters.*

HOWARD   Joan, can I have a word?

JOAN 4   No.

HOWARD   I...um...it's...We're having a baby. The BBC have
offered me a salary.

JOAN 4   'Crack!' went my heart.

HOWARD   There really isn't a /choice.

JOAN 4   /Choice? No. There really isn't.

HOWARD   I'm—

JOAN 4   Don't be. Promise you'll bring the princess to see me
when she's born. I've got an apple. Or a spinning wheel.
Or something.

> **HOWARD** *nods and exits.* ***MUSIC: "GOODBYE"***
> *(whistled Reprise) plays.* **MURRAY MELVIN** *enters,
> carrying a cup of tea. He hands it to* **JOAN 4**.

(to **MURRAY MELVIN***)* Thanks, darling. *(To* **AUDIENCE***)* Have
you met Murray? Adorable tea-maker and general source of
comfort. He's on a Cooperative apprenticeship. Two pounds
a week from them and Gerry matches it to tie in with the
rest of the wages, and we're going to find a part for him
any minute now, isn't that right, Murray?

MURRAY MELVIN   Yes, Joan. If you say so. *(To* **AUDIENCE***)* Hello
everybody. *(To* **JOAN 4***)* Anything else?

JOAN 4   *(to* **MURRAY MELVIN***)* Not at present. *(Sips tea.)* It's
perfect, Nut.

> **MURRAY MELVIN** *exits.*

(to **AUDIENCE***)* Next up in our new home we need new voices.
And you know me: I want only the truly disenfranchised

to grace our stage. First up: The Irish. Mr Brendan Behan. His first play? The Quare Fellow.

Year counter counts up to 1956. **ROSALIE** *enters at speed.*

ROSALIE Sorry to interrupt. *(To* **AUDIENCE***)* Sorry, everybody. *(To* **JOAN 4***)* It's Brendan.

JOAN 4 Where is he?

ROSALIE In the pub.

JOAN 4 Well, send Gerry over..

ROSALIE In Dublin.

JOAN 4 With the script.

ROSALIE Yes. Gerry sent his fare. Brendan drank it. Gerry sent it again. So, in the meantime...

JOAN 4 Company!

COMPANY *appears.*

A prison yard, Dublin. Dawn fatigues. Execution Day. Harry, you're the screw.

HARRY Pick up the fag ends, boys.********

PRISONER 1 Oy! The girls are hanging the laundry. A mere glimpse of those damp undergarments and I'm a flagpole.

HARRY *(To* **PRISONER 1***)* Oy! Down. *(To* **ALL***)* The rest of you, look lively The silver-topped cane has been granted a reprieve.

PRISONER 2 But the pauper will hang.

HARRY Let that be a lesson to you all.

PRISONER 2 Aye. That'll learn him to be born poor.

JOAN 4 The hangman tends the noose as a midwife her forceps. Jimmie? A song.

******** Harry and the prisoners speak in Dublin accents.

The COMPANY *improvises silently whilst* JIMMIE MILLER *sings a capella.*

[MUSIC NO. 15A: "TOP OF THE MORNING"]

JIMMIE MILLER

> TOP OF THE MORNING TO THE MEN IMPRISONED FOR THEIR CRIME
> TOP OF THE MORNING TO THE MEN WHO HANG BEFORE THEIR TIME
> TOP OF THE MORNING ALSO TO MY MOTHER'S BLEEDING HEART
> AS THEY SHOVED ME INTO BORSTAL WHEN MY LIFE WAS AT ITS START

ROSALIE *rushes on, carrying an envelope.*

ROSALIE Remember I told you Gerry had sent Brendan's fare?

JOAN 4 Twice.

ROSALIE Brendan /drank it twice.

JOAN 4 /Drank it twice. Gerry's an /idiot.

ROSALIE /Gerry's learning. This time he sent a ticket, and Brendan arrives next week. Meanwhile, this arrived. (ROSALIE *hands* JOAN 4 *the envelope*) Postmark says "Manchester".

As JOAN 4 *opens it, the year counter counts up to 1958. Music starts:* SONG: "A TASTE OF HONEY". SHELAGH DELANEY *enters. The characters in her song are acted out by* THE COMPANY, *with* MURRAY MELVIN *taking the part of* GEOFFREY, *and the projector showing images of the show's success.* BACKING VOCALISTS, *played by members of* THE COMPANY.

[MUSIC NO. 16: "A TASTE OF HONEY"]

Music: The sound of a typewriter.

SHELAGH DELANEY

DEAR MISS LITTLEWOOD,
I'M NINETEEN YEARS OLD
I WRITE TO YOU FROM SALFORD WHERE IT'S RAINY AND COLD
I HOPE YOU WON'T CONSIDER ME OUTRAGEOUSLY BOLD...

TWO WEEKS AGO I SAW MY VERY FIRST PLAY
IT WASN'T THAT IMPRESSIVE I AM SORRY TO SAY
I KNEW I COULD DO BETTER SO THE VERY NEXT DAY
I STARTED WRITING THE ENCLOSED.

IT'S CALLED 'A TASTE OF HONEY'

BACKING VOCALISTS

A TASTE OF HONEY

SHELAGH DELANEY

ALL ABOUT A TEEN WHO GETS KNOCKED UP BY AN ITINERANT
    SAILOR
FOR A TASTE OF HONEY

BACKING VOCALISTS

A TASTE – OOH! – A TASTE OF HONEY

SHELAGH DELANEY

OTHERWISE HER LIFE WILL JUST BE BORING AND STALE,

ALL *(spoken)* Right?

SHELAGH DELANEY

(sung) IT'S GOT A MUM CALLED HELEN

BACKING VOCALISTS

MUM! A WAYWARD WOMAN!

SHELAGH DELANEY

HER BOYFRIEND CALLED PETER

BACKING VOCALISTS

A WIDE BOY!

SHELAGH DELANEY

OUR TEEN CALLED JO WHO'S GOT A RED HOT SAILOR IN TOW

BACKING VOCALISTS

OOH, OOH, OOH, OOH, OOH, OOH...

SHELAGH DELANEY

AND THEN THERE'S GEOFFREY:

BACKING VOCALISTS

AND THEN THERE'S GEOFFREY, OOH: GEOFFREY! OOH...

SHELAGH DELANEY

KINDNESS AND DEVOTION COMBINED...

BACKING VOCALISTS

GEOFFREY! OOH...

SHELAGH DELANEY

OH, YEAH, THERE'S GEOFFREY, WHO, I THINK YOU SHOULD
KNOW IS NOT THE MARRYING KIND...

BACKING VOCALISTS

MMM!

SHELAGH DELANEY

I HOPE IT'S GOT SOME MERIT AND IT ISN'T TOO DAFT

BACKING VOCALISTS

MMM-HMM

SHELAGH DELANEY

I'M WILLING AND INTELLIGENT AND EAGER TO GRAFT

BACKING VOCALISTS

MMM-HMM

SHELAGH DELANEY

I KNOW IT ISN'T FAULTLESS BUT IT'S JUST A FIRST DRAFT...

BACKING VOCALISTS

GOD, WE REALLY HOPE YOU LIKE

SHELAGH DELANEY

I HOPE YOU LIKE 'A TASTE OF HO-NEY'

BACKING VOCALISTS

A TASTE OF HONEY

MMM-HMM.

SHELAGH DELANEY *(spoken)*
YOURS SINCERELY, SHELAGH DELANEY.

Song ends.

JOAN 4 Gerry'll sort the contract, darling. Second floor, door on the right.

JIMMIE MILLER *enters.*

JIMMIE MILLER Joan?

JOAN 4 Jimmie.

JIMMIE MILLER I've been having a think. I'm leaving.

JOAN 4 Yes.

JIMMIE MILLER It's the programming, Joan. Crowd pleasers. Prickteasers.

JOAN 4 A Taste of Honey, a prickteaser? Really? An unmarried, white teenager becomes pregnant with the child of a black sailor? He buggers /off—

JIMMIE MILLER /I've seen the play, /Joan...

JOAN 4 /Leaving the child to be brought up by a househusband of indeterminate sexual preference? It's hardly The Belles of St Trinians, is it, Jimmie? It's about what it is to be a woman – or, what it is, not to be a man. Perhaps that's the problem. That the show by a teenage prodigy from Salford is the one that finally puts us on the front page? That's going to smart. I sympathise. And that this particular genius is a) not you; b) a woman, and c) one who has the temerity not to worship your penis, well that's a bitter pill, I can see that. But I'll let you in on a secret, Jimmie: you were sodding marvellous. Unheard, unseen: who cares? We had a marvellous time. We were a marvellous time. And this gittish jealousy is corrosive. We may never be babes again, Jimmie, but we can still, at least, be midwives.

JIMMIE MILLER The Hootenannies want me.

JOAN 4 The folk fuckers? Terrific. May they worship you as you truly deserve to be worshipped.

JIMMIE MILLER Gerry's not worthy of /you.

JOAN 4 /Goodbye, Jimmie.

JIMMIE MILLER Goodbye, Joan.

They hug. **JOAN 4** *kisses him fondly.* **JIMMIE MILLER** *exits.* ***MUSIC: "THE HONEY/HOSTAGE JIG"*** *underscore. The* **COMPANY** *rehearse an Irish jig as though in preparation for the opening scene of Brendan Behan's The Hostage.* **ROSALIE** *enters.*

ROSALIE Everything alright, Joan?

JOAN 4 Yes. Where's Brendan?

ROSALIE He's in the building.

JOAN 4 Tell me he's not in the bar.

ROSALIE He said he was thirsty.

JOAN LITTLEWOOD *(to* **AUDIENCE***)* The Hostage was brilliant. A smash hit. Paris, West End, Broadway: unanimous.

JOAN 4 *(to* **COMPANY***)* Tea break.

ROSALIE Good, because you've got a meeting with the Arts Council.

ROSALIE *winces and runs off as* **JOAN LITTLEWOOD** *enters as the* **ARTS COUNCIL.**

JOAN LITTLEWOOD Time. Trouble. Application. Base.

JOAN 4 We've got a base!

JOAN LITTLEWOOD Ethically averse. In no way precludes you.

JOAN 4 Oh, fuck off.

JOAN LITTLEWOOD Brilliant.

JOAN LITTLEWOOD *exits as* **GERRY RAFFLES** *enters with an envelope.*

GERRY RAFFLES The Arts Council is giving the Royal Court five grand. They're giving us: one. I say, I say, I say, what do you call a theatre company based in Chelsea?

JOAN 4 Spoilt.

GERRY RAFFLES *hands* **JOAN 4** *the envelope.*

GERRY RAFFLES Someone called Frank Norman. Postmark: Soho.

JOAN 4 *opens the envelope, withdraws a letter and reads. Music starts.* **FRANK NORMAN** *appears.*

[MUSIC NO. 17: "A TASTE OF HONEY" *(Reprise: Frank Norman)]*

FRANK NORMAN
DEAR MISS LITTLEWOOD, I'M NINETEEN YEARS OLD
I WRITE TO YOU FROM SOHO, WHERE IT'S RAINY AND COLD
I HAD A STRETCH IN PRISON BUT WAS LATELY PAROLED
AND STARTED WRITING THE ENCLOSED

IT'S CALLED 'FINGS AIN'T WOT THEY USED TO BE'
IT'S ALL ABOUT A GAMBLER WHO IS DOWN ON HIS LUCK
WHO SAYS "FINGS AIN'T WOT THEY USED T'BE,
'CAUSE NOW THEY SAY 'A MASSAGE', INSTEAD OF A F -"/

Music continues (vamp).

JOAN 4 /Frank, darling, it's terribly promising, but it needs songs. There's a chap called Lionel Bart I want you to meet. Lionel?

Enter **LIONEL BART.**

Frank: Lionel. He's a songwriter. Lionel: Frank. Now carry on from where you left off.

The characters in the song are acted out by **THE COMPANY**, *with* **MURRAY MELVIN** *taking the part of the designer.*

LIONEL IT'S GOT A GUY –

FRANK CALLED FREDDIE

LIONEL A GIRL –

FRANK CALLED LILY

LIONEL A SERGEANT –

FRANK CALLED COLLINS

LIONEL A TOFF –

FRANK CALLED PERCY;

FRANK and **LIONEL**

SOME HOOKERS AND SOME BUILDERS
AND SOME COPS YOU REALLY CAN'T TRUST

OOH!!

PLUS A DESIGNER
OOH YEAH!

LIONEL BART

OOH...

FRANK NORMAN

TALENTED, BUT OFTEN MALIGNED

LIONEL BART

OOH...

FRANK NORMAN and **LIONEL BART**

YES: A DESIGNER, WHO YOU'VE PROBABLY SUSSED
IS NOT THE MARRYING KIND...

IT'S CALLED 'FINGS AIN'T WOT THEY USED TO BE'
IT'S LIKE A TALKING PICTURE OF THE REAL EAST END,
WHICH SAYS: "FINGS AIN'T WHAT THEY USED T'BE!"

End of song. **FRANK NORMAN, LIONEL BART** *and the* **COMPANY** *exit. Year counter counts up to 1959.* **JOAN 4** *puts on* **BARBARA YOUNG**'s *coat from Act One.* **MURRAY MELVIN** *enters.*

MURRAY MELVIN Joan?

JOAN 4 Murray.

MURRAY MELVIN It's Gerry. He's in his office. The new girl.

JOAN 4 I hate a tattle-tale. Gerry's and my private life is just that, even when he insists on making it public. No good will come from playing my herald, understood?

MURRAY MELVIN Yes, Joan.

> **MURRAY MELVIN** *exits.* **GERRY RAFFLES** *enters.*

JOAN 4 Gerry.

GERRY RAFFLES Dry cleaning collected: jumpers ready for winter.

JOAN 4 Good.

GERRY RAFFLES Steak for supper?

JOAN 4 Yes.

GERRY RAFFLES Sorted the contracts for Fings.

JOAN 4 Right.

GERRY RAFFLES Oh, and Joan?

JOAN 4 Yes?

GERRY RAFFLES The Arts Council.

JOAN 4 Forewarned.

> *Enter* **JOAN LITTLEWOOD** *as the* **ARTS COUNCIL**.

JOAN LITTLEWOOD And now that you're successful, of course, you'll no longer need us.

JOAN 4 Get away from me.

> **JOAN LITTLEWOOD** *exits.* **VICTOR SPINETTI** *enters wearing a long fur coat, brought in by* **MURRAY MELVIN**.

VICTOR SPINETTI I say, I say, I say, what do you call a theatre company based in East fifteen?

JOAN 4 Underfunded.

VICTOR SPINETTI I've come about the theatre.

JOAN 4 Name?

VICTOR SPINETTI Spinetti. Victor Spinetti.

> **JOAN 4** *strokes* **VICTOR SPINETTI***'s coat.*

JOAN 4 Welcome, Victor; Murray, make the tea.

> **MURRAY MELVIN** *exits with* **VICTOR SPINETTI. BARBARA YOUNG** *enters.*

BARBARA YOUNG Joan. Can I have a word?

JOAN 4 Barbara.

BARBARA YOUNG I wanted to tell you that I'll be leaving at the end of the season.

JOAN 4 I could smell it.

BARBARA YOUNG It's the BBC. They've offered me a series.

JOAN 4 Well, you may find happiness as a woman, but – outside of my company – you'll never find satisfaction as an artist.

BARBARA YOUNG Can I have my coat back?

> **JOAN 4** *pulls the coat around her.*

JOAN 4 What coat?

> **BARBARA YOUNG** *shrugs and exits. Year counter counts up to 1960.*

> **GERRY RAFFLES** *enters, carrying an envelope.*

If you tell me you're leaving, I'll punch you.

GERRY RAFFLES So flirtatious, as ever. No, I'm not leaving. But I did buy a boat.

JOAN 4 A boat? Now? Really?

GERRY RAFFLES I thought we might have fun. Sailing. South of France.

JOAN 4 I hate sailing. Sounds idyllic.

> **GERRY RAFFLES** *hands* **JOAN 4** *the envelope.*

GERRY RAFFLES This arrived. Someone called Hal Prince. Postmark: New York...

> **JOAN 4** *opens the envelope, removes the letter and reads. Music starts.* **HAL PRINCE** *enters. Year counter counts up to 1961.* **BACKING VOCALISTS** *played by* **THE COMPANY**.

> ***[MUSIC NO. 18: "A TASTE OF HONEY" (Reprise: Hal Prince)]***

HAL PRINCE
DEAR MISS LITTLEWOOD, I'M THIRTY YEARS OLD
I WRITE TO YOU FROM BROADWAY WHERE IT'S RAINY AND COLD
I SAW YOUR SHOW, 'THE HOSTAGE' AND WAS TOTALLY SOLD
AND SO I'M SENDING THE ENCLOSED

> **JOAN LITTLEWOOD** *enters, enthusiastically joins in the dancing and encourages the* **COMPANY** *to join in, too, as backing vocalists acting out* **HAL PRINCE***'s song.*

	BACKING VOCALS
IT'S CALLED 'THEY MIGHT BE GIANTS'	IT'S CALLED 'THEY MIGHT BE GIANTS'
FIRST REFUSAL:	TELL HIM YOUR THOUGHTS:
HAVE A READ AND TELL ME YOUR THOUGHTS	
'THEY MIGHT BE GIANTS'	'MIGHT BE GIANTS'

HAL PRINCE and BACKING VOCALS
'CAUSE IF YOU WANT IT, THEN I'LL JOIN UP THE DOTS

BACKING VOCALISTS
IF YOU WANT IT, THEN HE'LL JOIN UP THE DOTS.

HAL PRINCE
IT'S GOT A SHRINK CALLED WATSON

JOAN LITTLEWOOD
A SHRINK CALLED WATSON;

HAL PRINCE
A HERO, CALLED JUSTIN;

JOAN LITTLEWOOD
A HERO CALLED JUSTIN;

HAL PRINCE
HE'S A GRIEVING WIDOWER CONVINCED HE'S SHERLOCK
    HOLMES

JOAN LITTLEWOOD
SHERLOCK HOLMES: OOH!

HAL PRINCE
THEN THERE'S HIS BROTHER...

JOAN LITTLEWOOD
GO ON AND TELL ME ALL ABOUT IT, HAL!

HAL PRINCE
CURSED WITH A MALEVOLENT MIND...

ROSALIE *enters and interrupts. The song comes to an abrupt halt.*

ROSALIE Hal: I'm sorry to interrupt. Joan.

JOAN LITTLEWOOD Oh, what?.

ROSALIE 'They Might Be Giants' was terrible. A humiliating flop. Look, it's one thing not letting the truth get in the way of a good story, it's a whole other thing, telling a barefaced lie just because you know what comes next. So don't parade around celebrating it or I'll pull the plug. *(To* **HAL***)* Now please don't think us rude, Hal, and feel free to stay for the rest of the show. But we need to press on. Avis, would you mind...?

AVIS BUNNAGE *(to* **HAL PRINCE***)* I'll show you to the bar. Mine's a port and lemon. We'll find a cosy little nook.********

> **HAL PRINCE** *exits with* **AVIS BUNNAGE**. **JOAN 4** *removes the cap and hands it to* **JOAN LITTLEWOOD**.

JOAN 4 I don't want to be Joan anymore.

JOAN LITTLEWOOD I know the feeling.

> **ROSALIE** *looks expectantly at* **JOAN LITTLEWOOD**. **JOAN LITTLEWOOD** *wolf-whistles*. **JOAN 5** *enters*. **JOAN LITTLEWOOD** *hands the cap to* **JOAN 5**.

I age.

JOAN 5 Who doesn't?

JOAN LITTLEWOOD The dead. *(To* **AUDIENCE***)* And now: How Home is Where the Art is, or, When, For Your Ongoing Delectation, I Fuck It All Up. I thank you. And a round of applause for the lovely Rosalie.

> **JOAN LITTLEWOOD** *applauds* **ROSALIE**. *Exeunt.*

******** See earlier footnotes on Avis's pronunciation.

Scene Twenty One

*June, 1961. **GERRY RAFFLES**'s office, the Theatre Royal, Stratford East. There is a commotion coming from behind a cupboard door – grunting and banging. Enter **JOAN 5**, who is wearing a kilt and heavy sailor's sweater with a fur-lined mackintosh around her shoulders. She exudes confidence.*

JOAN 5 Gerry?

GERRY RAFFLES *(from inside the cupboard, on the brink of orgasm)* Just a minute!

JOAN 5 I need to tell you something.

GERRY RAFFLES Be right there!

JOAN 5 Finish presently, would you, Gerry? I haven't got all day.

*   **GERRY RAFFLES** *emerges doing up his flies followed shortly afterwards by a **YOUNG WOMAN** adjusting her clothing.*

YOUNG WOMAN I'm—

JOAN 5 Barbara?

YOUNG WOMAN *(to **GERRY RAFFLES**)* That was lovely.

*   **YOUNG WOMAN** *exits.*

GERRY RAFFLES Sorry you witnessed that.

JOAN 5 I chose to. It sharpened my resolve. I'm leaving.

GERRY RAFFLES She's just a—

JOAN 5 A Barbara?

GERRY RAFFLES A blip. Is this about *Giants*? It's just a show, Joan. A shitty show. Cynical critics. We'll make another. We'll get through. We're stable, now. More than we ever thought possible. The West End transfers... Broadway...

JOAN 5 America: the land of the indiscriminate standing ovation.

GERRY RAFFLES This is home, Joan. Don't blow it. Not now.

JOAN 5 A threat? Never underestimate my appetite for uproar,
Gerry. When you're emasculated by my risen star, you grab
the nearest Barbara and fondle her tits: is that what you
mean by "home"? You can keep it. Everything has gone
wrong. Art isn't flashbulbs and furs, Gerry. It's graft and
grit. It grows in the cracks. And we're in a greenhouse, and
it's going to take some shattering. Your West End transfers
are pickling my shows. They are just for tourists: Madame
Tussaud's, Buckingham Palace, Joan's Latest Offering: tick,
tick, tick. Is that what you mean by "stable"? We used to
make theatre for the self-effacing and the disenfranchised.
Here, we make it for the critics, measure our worth by the
box office, and give the poor a difficult sightline. Jimmie
was right. And where are the actors that lived together, and
crafted together? Those gits at the BBC have plundered my
casts so that I have to construct a troupe from scratch every
fucking time. This city – this theatre – is dead. And we are
dead, Gerry. Dead. I sometimes feel as though I've been
peeled and then just shoved outside in the endless weather.

GERRY RAFFLES Joan—

JOAN 5 No, Gerry. I've met someone.

GERRY RAFFLES What?

JOAN 5 You can fuck an actress in the stationery cupboard but
I can't fall in love?

GERRY RAFFLES She's immaterial.

JOAN 5 You say it like it's a solution, Gerry, when what you're
actually doing, when you say that, is demeaning everyone
you fuck: we're all immaterial. Which makes you a cunt.
And it's so fucking sordid, Gerry.

GERRY RAFFLES Who is he?

JOAN 5 An architect. He inspires me. Either that, or your incontinent concupiscence has finally worn me down. I used to be a radical, Now I'm a cliché.

GERRY RAFFLES Sometimes the most radical thing you can do is to commit.

JOAN 5 Ha! That's good. No irony, Gerry?

GERRY RAFFLES Where will you go?

JOAN 5 Maybe I'll find something in Paris, where it began for me, some stones to throw. Or I'll go to Africa, where everything began. Word has it, they have excellent rocks.

GERRY RAFFLES The things I've learned about you, Joan, are that you need someone who will pick up your clothes, cook your meals. You can't be alone.

JOAN 5 Two things I learned from you, Gerry: I'm always alone, and I'm never at home.

GERRY RAFFLES All my energy comes from you.

JOAN 5 Bullseye, Gerry: you sap me.

[MUSIC NO. 19: "CHANGE"]

I'M NOT SOMETHING YOU CAN TAKE IN YOUR HAND
AND KEEP IN YOUR POCKET
AND UNDERSTAND
I'M NOT
I'M NOT SOMEONE YOU CAN PRIMP AND PREEN AND POLISH
    AND CLEAN AND UNDERSTAND: I'M NOT
I CHANGE LIKE THE WEATHER
I'M SKITTISH LIKE THAT
I CHANGE MY MIND LIKE SOME FOLK CHANGE THEIR HAT
I CHANGE LIKE THE WEATHER
I'M BRITISH LIKE THAT
NEVER ACCEPT, OR YOU'LL GET TRAPPED.
SIMPLY BECOME MORE ADEPT AT ADAPTING

QUICK: OUT OF THE TRAPS, JOAN
OFF WITH THE TIES THAT BIND

LEAVE ALL THOSE LIES BEHIND TO FIND A TRUE WORLD
OUT OF THE TRAPS, JOAN, AND FLY!

FLY OUT OF THE TRAPS, JOAN,
PULL OUT AND LET 'EM ROT!
STICKING WITH WHAT YOU'VE GOT IS NOT A NEW WORLD
LET IT COLLAPSE, JOAN, AND FLY!

JOAN 5 *is joined by* **JOAN 1, JOAN 2, JOAN 3, JOAN 4** *and* **JOAN LITTLEWOOD.** *All sung simultaneously.*

JOAN 3	CHANGE IS NOT AN OPTION; IT'S THE NATURE OF LIFE/
JOAN LITTLEWOOD	WHAT WAS I THINKING, GERRY?
JOAN 5	I CHANGE, LIKE THE WEATHER: I'M SKITTISH LIKE THAT
JOAN 4	NOW IS THE ONLY THING TO BEAR
JOAN 1	I'M JOAN, JOAN ALL ALONE FROM MY HEAD TO MY TOES
JOAN 2	MY OLD MAN IS HANDSOME

JOAN LITTLEWOOD	I'LL NEVER FORGIVE MYSELF WHO WAS I KIDDING, GERRY?
JOAN 4	THE SPARK OF INVENTION THE BONE OF CONTENTION
JOAN 3	CHANGE IS NEITHER PRIVILEGE NOR CURSE
JOAN 2	MY OLD MAN IS SAD HE HAD TO LEAVE ME BEHIND HE'LL SAY: "JOAN, YOU'VE NOTHING TO HIDE."
JOAN 1	IF NOBODY LOVES ME, WHAT DO I CARE?
JOAN 5	I CHANGE MY MIND LIKE SOME FOLK CHANGE THEIR HAT

JOAN LITTLEWOOD and **JOANS 1-4**

JOAN ALL ALONE *(staggered)*
JOAN ALL ALONE AND FOR WHAT?

JOAN 5   JOAN ALL ALONE, ALL
                                    ALONE
                                    I CHANGE LIKE THE
                                    WEATHER: I'M
                                    BRITISH LIKE THAT
JOAN LITTLEWOOD   IF ONLY I COULD TAKE
                                    THINGS BACK

JOAN 4   THE PAST LIES IN
                                    TATTERS...

JOAN 1   BUT IF, SOMEDAY,
                                    SOMEONE SHOULD
                                    APPEAR
JOAN 2   AND ONE DAY, SOMEDAY,
                                    MY OLD MAN WILL
                                    ARRIVE
JOAN 3   STRANGE THAT
                                    SOMETIMES CHANGE
                                    ITSELF REQUIRES A
                                    NUDGE...

JOAN LITTLEWOOD, JOAN 1   JOAN ALL ALONE!
    and **JOAN 2 JOAN 3**

JOAN 4   WELL, ANYHOW

JOAN 3   ...OR A SHOVE

ALL JOANS
> JOAN ALL ALONE!

GERRY RAFFLES
> GO, BEFORE YOU MAKE THE WHOLE THING WORSE!

> **GERRY RAFFLES** *gradually exits through the following.*
> **JOAN LITTLEWOOD** *remains, but watches him go.*

JOAN 1
> QUICK!

JOAN 2
> QUICK!

JOAN 3
> QUICK!

JOAN 4
> QUICK!

JOAN 5
> QUICK

JOAN 1 and **JOAN 2**
> QUICK! QUICK!

JOAN 3 and **JOAN 4**
> QUICK! QUICK!

JOAN 5	QUICK: OUT OF THE TRAPS, JOAN; OFF WITH THE TIES THAT BIND
JOAN 4	QUICK: OUT OF THE TRAPS; OFF WITH THE TIES THAT BIND
JOAN 3	QUICK: OUT OF THE TRAPS AND THE TIES THAT BIND
JOAN 1 and **JOAN 2**	QUICK: OFF WITH THE TIES THAT BIND

JOAN 1-5

LEAVE ALL THOSE LIES BEHIND TO FIND A TRUE WORLD

JOAN 5	OUT OF THE TRAPS, JOAN
JOAN 4	OUT OF THE TRAPS, JOAN
JOAN 3	OUT OF THE TRAPS, JOAN
JOAN 2	OUT OF THE TRAPS, JOAN
JOAN 1	OUT OF THE TRAPS
JOAN 2-5	AND GOODBYE!

JOAN 1	AND GOODBYE!
JOAN 4	GOODBYE!
JOAN 3	GOODBYE!
JOAN 1	GOODBYE!

JOAN 2 and **JOAN 5**	GOODBYE!
JOAN 4	GOODBYE!
JOAN 3	GOODBYE!
JOAN 1	GOODBYE!

JOAN 1–5
GOODBYE!

End of song. Year counter counts up to 1962.

Scene Twenty Two

[SONG: "PARIS IS A WOMAN" (Reprise: Underscore)]

JOAN LITTLEWOOD It's 1962. I'm in Paris, with the architect. Name: Cedric Price. I don't age in Paris. I don't believe anyone ever has. How To Be Away From Home When It Really Sodding Counts.

Paris. A balcony overlooking the Seine, a bedroom just visible behind. A more up-market version of the one shared by **JOAN 2** *and* **NICK** *in Act One.* **JOAN 5** *and* **CEDRIC PRICE** *are post-coital, sitting sharing a cigarette and a glass of wine.*

JOAN 5 This place where anyone can come and learn anything they like, it's a university of the streets: you name it, there'd be a class for it, or just come along and work out how best to willingly waste your time in it.

CEDRIC PRICE I'll design it, you fill it.

JOAN 5 What'll we call it?

CEDRIC takes a long, languorous drag on the cigarette and thinks.

CEDRIC PRICE The Affair of the Century?

JOAN 5 The building, you idiot.

CEDRIC PRICE The Palace of Varieties?

JOAN 5 Been there, done that.

CEDRIC PRICE The Pleasure Gardens.

JOAN 5 Unoriginal. That's no fun.

CEDRIC PRICE The House of Fun?

JOAN 5 Sounds like a fairground. The Fun House?

CEDRIC PRICE Is a kindergarten. It needs to be grand, palatial.

JOAN 5 Palace? /The Fun Palace!

CEDRIC PRICE /The Fun Palace! What'll we call it? Us, I mean.

JOAN 5 No: I'm not doing that.

> **JOAN 5** *moves to head inside, away from the* **AUDIENCE**.

Come: let's fornicate our bleeding lives away.

> *There is a knock at the door. A* **BELLBOY** *enters carrying a telegram.*

BELLBOY Télégramme pour Mademoiselle Petitbois.

> *The* **BELLBOY** *hands the telegram to* **JOAN 5**. *As she opens it, it bursts into flames, and we hear the sudden sound of a raging fire. Flames engulf the screen. Year counter counts up to 1963. Screen shows a Telegram with the following text: GERRY ALIVE STOP FIRE ON BOAT STOP HURRY HOME STOP.*

Scene Twenty Three

A hospital. A burns unit. **GERRY RAFFLES** *is in a hospital bed, his torso and lower limbs covered with a frame.* **JOAN 1, JOAN 2, JOAN 3, JOAN 4, JOAN 5** *and* **JOAN LITTLEWOOD** *are at his bedside.* **ALL JOANS** *act seamlessly, as though a single actor. There is a copy of* The Donkeys *in* **GERRY RAFFLES***'s lap.*

JOAN 5 I'll never forgive myself.

GERRY RAFFLES You never wanted me to go on that yacht.

JOAN 4 Don't call it a yacht. They'll think we're middle class. If I hadn't left I'd've been able to nag you.

GERRY RAFFLES I've missed your nagging.

JOAN 2 Mmm.

GERRY RAFFLES Are you coming home?

JOAN 4 With a few major adjustments.

GERRY RAFFLES Where is your art?

JOAN LITTLEWOOD Where you are, Gerry. Where you are.

GERRY RAFFLES Still with that rackety architect?

JOAN 2 Periodically.

GERRY RAFFLES Working on...?

JOAN 1 A Fun Palace.

GERRY RAFFLES Haven't you already done that in Stratford? Read this. *(He hands her* The Donkeys*)* And then tell me why you're not making it into a show. Like 'Last Edition', only for the First World War. Songs, montages, news announcements. You know the drill. Pun intended.

JOAN 3 How we met.

GERRY RAFFLES How you ignited my passion. I've done little else but listen to the radio. Chap called Charles Chilton did a piece called "The Long, Long Trail". Songs from the Great War. Here's the recording. I've contacted him to talk about turning it into something. The songs are marvellous.

GERRY RAFFLES *sings a well-known soldiers' song from the First World War in advanced RP.* **JOAN LITTLEWOOD** *joins in.*

JOAN 2 No, no, no: we can't have all those BBC vowels.

GERRY RAFFLES It hurts when I laugh.

JOAN LITTLEWOOD Sorry.

GERRY RAFFLES You'll do it?

JOAN 5 You've been busy.

GERRY RAFFLES I'm almost entirely a complete and utter capitalist wanker, Joan. Greedy in all areas. But the minuscule part of me that isn't, remains capable of listening. Besides, I know which side my bread's buttered. Nothing's the same without you. And that includes the West End. It stinks to high heaven, these days. Stinks.

JOAN 4 Don't expect me to freshen it up.

GERRY RAFFLES Throw a few stones, would you?

JOAN 2 I've been collecting them. How's the company?

GERRY RAFFLES What company? We start auditioning tomorrow. Here's your list. Ten o'clock, sharp.

JOAN 3 They'll let you out of here?

GERRY RAFFLES I've found myself a very understanding nurse.

ALL JOANS Ha ha.

GERRY RAFFLES You're different.

JOAN 5 I've gone back to my roots. I've pulled myselves together.

GERRY RAFFLES *(laughing)* It suits you. Ouch. Joan?

ALL JOANS Yes?

GERRY RAFFLES Diabetes.

JOAN 4 They confirmed it.

GERRY RAFFLES We'll manage.

JOAN LITTLEWOOD Scene 24: How Not Every Barbara is a Potential Threat.

Scene Twenty Four

Outside a stage door. **JOAN 6** *is sitting smoking a cigarette, a mop in the other hand.* **BARBARA WINDSOR** *enters.*

BARBARA WINDSOR Hello. I've come about the theatre.

JOAN 6 Name?

BARBARA WINDSOR Barbara. Barbara Windsor. Like the queen.

JOAN 6 I thought she was called Elizabeth. Where have you come from, darling?

BARBARA WINDSOR Stoke Newington. But I stayed at a mate's flat last night.

JOAN 6 Nervous?

BARBARA WINDSOR No. I don't really want the job, to be honest. My mum worked her arse off to get us out of the East End, so this is the last place I'd want to work. But my mate Lionel recommended me to them and when I got the call for an audition, I thought...

JOAN 6 You'd do them a favour.

BARBARA WINDSOR Oh, don't be silly.

MURRAY MELVIN *enters.*

MURRAY MELVIN Barbara, is it?

BARBARA WINDSOR That's right.

MURRAY MELVIN Follow me.

JOAN 6 Give 'em hell. She's a right tyrant, that Littlewood bird.

BARBARA WINDSOR So I've heard. Nice meeting you.

BARBARA WINDSOR *follows* **MURRAY MELVIN**. **JOAN 6** *walks into the auditorium where she is joined by* **GERRY**

RAFFLES. BARBARA WINDSOR *steps into a spotlight, peers out into the auditorium, then shrugs.*

(spoken) Here's a little tip my daddy gave me:

[MUSIC NO. 20: "A LITTLE BIT OF BUSINESS"]

(sung) "WHEN THINGS ARE GOING FINE, ON THE SUNNY SIDE OF THE STAGE
YOU'LL FIND THAT PEOPLE SMILE AT YOU AND WAVE
THEY MAY THROW YOU A LOLLIPOP THEY MAY BUY YOU A DRINK
BUT YOU'LL FIND THEY ACT QUITE DIFFERENTLY IF THINGS GO ON THE BLINK
WHEN SHADOWS FALL AND AUDIENCES MUTTER
DON'T LET THEM DRAG YOU DOWN IN THE GUTTER...

JUST TAKE A BREATH
FIND YOUR LIGHT
SHOULDERS BACK AND LOOK THOSE PUNTERS IN THE EYES
THEY'VE ALL TURNED UP, SO THANK 'EM FOR THEIR PRESENCE
AND LET THEM KNOW THEY'RE IN FOR A SURPRISE
THEN, TO NAIL IT HOME, GOOD AND PROPER
AND TO MAKE SURE YOU TURN THAT FOE INTO A FRIEND
SING YOUR SONG, DANCE YOUR DANCE, BUT DON'T LEAVE NOTHING TO CHANCE
BY THROWING A BIT OF BUSINESS IN, RIGHT AT THE END

IF YOU CAN JUGGLE, THEN JUGGLE
IF YOU'VE GOT LEGS AND SUCH TO SHOW, GO ALL THE WAY
IF YOU'VE GOT THINGS THAT YOU CAN WIGGLE, MAKE THEM WIGGLE
AND THIS GAG'LL MAKE 'EM GIGGLE, BARBARA, DAY AFTER DAY
IF YOU GET IT RIGHT THE CROWDS WILL LOVE YOU
AND IF YOU DO IT TWICE, YOU'LL START A TREND
SO SHOULDERS BACK, FIND YOUR LIGHT, EYE TO EYE AND NIGHT BY NIGHT
JUST THROW A BIT OF BUSINESS IN, RIGHT AT THE END!"

NOW I'D LOVE TO JUGGLE BUT I'M NOT ABLE

AND I SEEM TO BE THE PROGENY OF ELVES

I HAVEN'T GOT THE LEGS OF BETTY GRABLE

AND THOSE THINGS THAT WIGGLE, TEND TO WIGGLE ALL BY
   THEMSELVES

BUT NOT MANY PEOPLE KNOW THAT I CAN CARTWHEEL

IT'S A LITTLE TRICK I DO FROM TIME TO TIME

IT'S NOT ALWAYS IN STYLE

BUT YOU'LL SEE WHY IT'S WORTHWHILE

'CAUSE A FROWN, TURNED UPSIDE DOWN, BECOMES A SMILE...

IT ISN'T FULL OF CLASS OR AIRS AND GRACES

BUT IT IS A SKILL ON WHICH I CAN DEPEND

AND I ALWAYS LOVE THE LOOK UPON YOUR FACES

WHEN I THROW MY BIT OF BUSINESS IN...

LITTLE BIT OF BUSINESS IN...

WHEN I THROW MY BIT OF BUSINESS IN, RIGHT AT THE END!

JOAN 6 *steps up on stage.*

[MUSIC NO. 21: "WHERE HAVE YOU BEEN ALL MY LIFE?" (Duet)]

JOAN 6

YOU

WHERE HAVE YOU BEEN ALL MY LIFE?

WHERE'VE YOU BEEN HIDING?

EVERYTHING I'VE EVER WANTED

EVERYTHING I'VE EVER DREAMED OF...

BARBARA WINDSOR *(spoken)* You're the cleaning lady!

JOAN 6 *(spoken)* I'm Joan Littlewood.

(sung) YOU

WHERE HAVE YOU BEEN ALL MY LIFE?

WHERE'VE YOU BEEN RESIDING?

YOU'RE APPLE PIE

YOU'RE WONDERFUL, OH

YOU

BARBARA WINDSOR

ME?

JOAN 6

WHERE HAVE YOU BEEN ALL THIS TIME?

BARBARA WINDSOR

WHERE HAVE I BEEN? NOWHERE SPECIAL, MISS
LITTLEWOOD...

JOAN 6

WHAT'VE YOU BEEN DOING?

BARBARA WINDSOR

NOTHING MUCH, APPARENTLY

JOAN 6

EVERYTHING I'D SET MY HEART ON

BARBARA WINDSOR

EVERYTHING, REALLY?

JOAN 6

EVERYTHING I'D EVER HOPED FOR, BARBARA

BARBARA WINDSOR

EVERYTHING, CLEARLY!

JOAN 6

NOW YOU'RE HERE AND WE'RE TOGETHER

BARBARA WINDSOR

I'M HERE, AND WE'RE TOGETHER

BOTH

WE'LL FLY TOGETHER, WE'LL FLY

JOAN 6

HERE WE'LL BE, I'LL TREAT YOU FONDLY

BARBARA WINDSOR

THERE, THERE...

JOAN 6

NO FEAR, TOGETHER, NO FEAR

BARBARA WINDSOR
HEAR, HEAR!

JOAN 6
YOU
WHERE HAVE YOU BEEN ALL THE WHILE?

BARBARA WINDSOR
STOKE NEWINGTON, LATTERLY...

JOAN 6
WHERE HAVE YOU BEEN WITH THAT SMILE?

BARBARA WINDSOR
SO MANY QUESTIONS!

JOAN 6
WILL YOU?

BARBARA WINDSOR
I FEEL WONDERFUL... *(She nods)*

JOAN 6 *(spoken)* Right: Gerry, sort out the contract, would you? And I know she's called Barbara and everything, but be sure to keep your hands to yourself with this one. See you Monday, Little Bird.

Song ends. **BARBARA WINDSOR** *exits on cloud nine. A* **REPORTER** *steps forward with a notebook.*

REPORTER The first day of rehearsals for your latest show: Tell me, Miss Littlewood: how does it feel to be back in Stratford?

JOAN 6 I never left.

REPORTER You went to Paris. For some months.

JOAN 6 Tell me Velasquez never worked on more than one canvas at a time.

JOAN 2 I travel.

JOAN 4 I diversify.

JOAN 3 I never abandon.

REPORTER I see. We asked Mr Noël Coward the following question: "Will success spoil Miss Littlewood?" Do you know his response?

JOAN 5 No.

REPORTER He said, "Will Miss Littlewood spoil success?" What do you say to that?

JOAN 6 Noël and I both grew up in south London. We both crossed the river to make a life for ourselves. He didn't make it much past the Strand, whilst I ended up marginally further north in a place called Salford. We know and respect each other, because of our differences as much as despite them. We relish the diversity of our various theatres. So don't try to pit us against each other, you drivel-peddling, bottom-feeder of a divot. Now if you don't mind, I've got a show to grow.

REPORTER *exits.*

JOAN LITTLEWOOD What was it I said earlier? "Change, and the world changes with you"? Well, what I learned next was: change history, and you change the world. Now, my friends: How To Take The Whole Fucking Globe By Storm. Company!

Scene Twenty Five

*[MUSIC NO. 22: "THE THEATRE WORKSHOP
STORY 4" (Reprise: Oh What a Lovely War)]*

The music begins under JOAN 6*'s speech and continues
under interspersed scenes.* JOAN 6 *is holding a script.*

JOAN 6   Research projects: go!

MURRAY MELVIN   Mustard gas: in World War I, the deployment
of mustard gas marked the first widespread use of/ chemical
weaponry. First used by the Germans in 1917 ...

BARBARA WINDSOR   /Recruitment: by August 1915, it was clear
that the war would continue far longer than/ originally
supposed, and that/ conscription was inevitable in order
to bolster numbers of soldiers on the front lines...

VICTOR SPINETTI   The Somme: July 1st, 1916, marked the first
day of the bloodiest battle in what was known at the time
as/ the Great War, with over 55,000 Allied casualities on
the first day, nearly 20,000 of which were fatalities.

AVIS BUNNAGE   /Mrs Pankhurst: at the outset of war, Emmeline
Pankhurst brokered a truce with the government granting
all suffragette prisoners their freedom./ She urged women
to join the war effort on the home front, domestically as
well as in the fields and the factories...

COMPANY
   /WE STUDY THE HISTORY OF WORLD WAR ONE INFANTRY
   AND DRAW THE CONCLUSION THEY WERE LIONS LED BY
      DONKEYS
   WE READ ABOUT SERBIA, RUSSIA AND GERMANY
   WE READ ABOUT SWITZERLAND, AND KITCHENER AND HAIG

BARBARA WINDSOR   Joan, we've been having a chat, backstage.
We've had enough. It's one thing saying you're putting on
a radical rewrite of history, but quite another getting us to
write the sodding thing for you. I – we – are really happy

to do a play about the first world war. Any play you like. You choose. Just one with a fucking script.

AVIS BUNNAGE Barbara...

JOAN 6 I've got this, thanks, Avis. It's a script you want, is it, Barbara? Do you know where Columbus was aiming for when he hit the New World?

BARBARA WINDSOR No.

JOAN 6 Japan. We're drawing the map, not reading it.

BARBARA WINDSOR Don't you come the ground-breaking explorer with me, Little Miss Littlewood. It won't wash. I don't buy your politics and I don't like your theatre. I'm off.

> **BARBARA WINDSOR** *goes to leave.* **THE COMPANY** *falters, deciding between* **JOAN 6** *and* **BARBARA WINDSOR**.

JOAN 6 What did your granddad do in the war, Barbara?

BARBARA WINDSOR What's it to you?

JOAN 6 Everything.

BARBARA WINDSOR British Expeditionary Force.

JOAN 6 Survived?

BARBARA YOUNG Physically.

JOAN 6 Murray?

MURRAY MELVIN British Transport.

JOAN 6 Rosalie?

ROSALIE Artists' Rifles.

JOAN 6 Avis?

AVIS BUNNAGE The Loyal Regiment.

JOAN 6 How topical. Is there a play about them? People like them, perhaps? It's not that I'm lazy, Barbara. I'll be up all night, every night with this one, just as I was with *Honey* and with *Fings*. Only with this show, I can't do it without you. Every single one of you. We're creating a theatrical monument. A monument that can be shared and seen by hundreds, perhaps thousands of people. A monument that can never be torn down. A monument to the faces that never made the front pages, to the voices that never made the radio, to the fireside tales that aren't recorded.

JOAN LITTLEWOOD *(sings)*

I DON'T WANT TO BE A SOLDIER;
I DON'T WANT TO GO TO WAR...

JOAN 6 As each veteran dies we lose a piece of our monument. Your monument. You're welcome to leave, Barbara. Any of you, for that matter. There shouldn't be a single person here who doesn't relish the opportunity to share their piece of history with our audiences. But Barbara: when you find yourself back in the familiar world of kicklines, and punchlines, just remember who we, over here, are doing it all for: the fallen and the forgotten.

BARBARA WINDSOR *rallies.*

Now then: how about we make a start on the songs? Remember, though: you're soldiers, not singers.

COMPANY

/WE LEARN ALL THE SONGS AND WE PRACTISE OUR DANCE
    ROUTINES

JOAN 6

I BRING IN A SERGEANT JUST TO LIVEN UP PROCEEDINGS

COMPANY

WE SCOUR OUR FAMILIES' PERSONAL HISTORIES
FOR PERTINENT STORIES TO ENHANCE THE COLD HARD
    FACTS

JOAN 6 Now where's that fucking projector? And the Pierrot costumes?

COMPANY
> WE USE A PROJECTOR FOR CONTEMPORARY IMAGES
> ABOVE IT A PANEL SHOWING FIGURES AND STATISTICS
> WE DRESS AS PIERROTS – LIKE SEASIDE COMEDIANS
> OUR AIM IS TO CHALLENGE AND TO ENTERTAIN AS ONE
>
> WE FASHION A SHOW OF WHIZZBANGS AND PETARDS
> A SHOW ABOUT SOLDIERS UP TO BAT
> A SHOW ABOUT GLOBAL TIT FOR TAT
> RETELLING THE WAR AS MUSIC-HALL CHARADES:
> WHENEVER YOU HAVE TO CHANGE YOUR CHARACTER, YOU
>   SIMPLY CHANGE YOUR HAT

JOAN 6 Spinoza? A word.

VICTOR SPINETTI *steps forward.*

You're mannered, stiff, and bordering on the inaudible.

VICTOR SPINETTI I never knew you cared.

JOAN 6 Bingo: that's the Victor I want on stage. Now: get out front before the opening number. "I say, I say, I say". Talk to them like they're just over the garden fence. You can ask questions, but be sure to wait for a response if you do. Liven them up.

VICTOR SPINETTI What with?

JOAN 6 Your scintillating personality and quickfire improvisations

VICTOR SPINETTI Yes, Joan.

JOAN 6 Oh, and Vic?

VICTOR SPINETTI Yes, Joan.

JOAN 6 Three things: if they can't laugh, they won't cry; don't use anything more than once, and don't make me say that twice.

VICTOR SPINETTI *grins, nods and exits.*

COMPANY

WE TELL OF THE DEVASTATION OF THE SOMME
WE TELL OF THE TOMMIES AND THE HUNS

AVIS BUNNAGE

AND THIRTY-ODD MILLION MOTHERS' SONS

COMPANY

WE SING AND WE DANCE, CONCLUDING WITH APLOMB:
THE SOLE BENEFICIARIES OF WARFARE ARE THE ONES WHO
    SELL THE GUNS

JOAN 6 Lights out. *(All lights are turned off)* Listen. The silence.
Christmas eve. No one move. *(Whispering)* Murray!

MURRAY MELVIN *and* **GERRY RAFFLES** *head to the back
of the stalls, and sing.*

MURRAY MELVIN

STILLE NACHT
HEILIGE NACHT
ALLES SCHLÄFT
EINSAM WACHT

COMPANY

WE PUT ON A SHOW TO HONOUR THE DECEASED
A SHOW FULL OF FURY AND COMPASSION
MARRYING PATHOS WITH PANACHE
THAT STARTS IN THE THEATRE ROYAL, STRATFORD EAST
AND TRAVELS TO BROADWAY VIA PARIS AS AN
    INTERNATIONAL...
(OH, OH, OH IT'S A LOVELY WAR!)
...SMASH!

Scene Twenty Six

Blackheath. **JOAN** *and* **GERRY RAFFLES***'s apartment.*
ALL JOAN*s are scattered around the seats, on the floor,
lurking in corners.* **GERRY RAFFLES** *enters. Music starts,
and the lyrics and spoken lines should intertwine with
minimal overlap. During the song, the year counter
counts up to 1975; projections take us through the decade
year by year, plus images and headlines: 'Joan's Fun
Palace Goes Ahead!' 'Arts Council Pulls the Plug on Joan's
Fun Palace!' 'Theatre Royal Due for Demolition!' 'Joan
Lies Down In Front of Bulldozers!' Finally: '1975: Gerry
Asks Joan to Join Him in France!' 'Joan Refuses. "I'm
Too Busy," She Says."*

[MUSIC NO. 23: "NOTHING MUCH HAPPENED AFTER THAT"]

JOAN 1

NOTHING MUCH HAPPENED AFTER THAT

GERRY RAFFLES Tunisia want a summer school.

JOAN 1

A CLOUDY SKY; A THREAT OF RAIN

JOAN 3 Let's go together.

JOAN 1

NOTHING MUCH HAPPENED AFTER THAT

GERRY RAFFLES Sweden want a few days lecturing at a
university.

JOAN 1

A BROKEN NAIL
A TWINGE OF PAIN

JOAN 2 I can fit that in.

JOAN 1

AND THAT WAS FINE

GERRY RAFFLES The Lovely War cast in America.

JOAN 1
    FINE

GERRY RAFFLES They need some TLC.

JOAN 1
    THAT WAS FINE

JOAN 4 Consider it done.

GERRY RAFFLES Avis has agreed to play Marie Lloyd.

JOAN 3 Super.

JOAN 2
    WE WERE JUST CHUNTERING ALONG

GERRY RAFFLES I was thinking...

JOAN 2
    ANOTHER SCRIPT
    ANOTHER PLAY

GERRY RAFFLES ...maybe we could take a break.

JOAN 2
    WHILE WE WERE CHUNTERING ALONG

GERRY RAFFLES You, me and the boat. South of France?

JOAN 2
    TO MY SURPRISE, I HAVE TO SAY

JOAN 5 You know how I hate that fucking boat.

JOAN 2
    THAT I WAS FINE

JOAN 5 Count me in.

JOAN 2
    FINE

    A telephone rings. **GERRY RAFFLES** *answers it.*

GERRY RAFFLES Hello? Speaking.

JOAN 2

> I WAS FINE.

GERRY RAFFLES Joan. It's Brendan.

JOAN 6 How is the old soak?

JOAN 3

> AFTER YOU GET WHAT YOU WANT, WHAT DO YOU DO WITH
> THE WANT?

GERRY RAFFLES He's dead.

JOAN 6 Oh.

JOAN 3

> PAT IT, AND PRICK IT, AND PUT IT AWAY ON A SHELF?

GERRY RAFFLES I'll get you a brandy.

> **GERRY RAFFLES** *exits.*

JOAN 4

> THE TRUTH IS, NO MATTER HOW SLYLY OR DEFTLY YOU TRY
> TO PRETEND,

> *A telephone rings.* **CEDRIC PRICE** *appears. Music
> continues.*

> YOU'RE NEVER AT HOME WITH YOURSELF

> **JOAN 3** *answers the telephone.*

JOAN 3 Blackheath 214?

CEDRIC PRICE Joan?

JOAN 3 Cedric.

JOAN 5

> THE TROUBLE WITH GETTING YOUR HEART'S DESIRE?

CEDRIC PRICE Are you busy?

JOAN 5

> CONTENTMENT'S A CONCEPT I DON'T UNDERSTAND.

JOAN 3 Barely.

JOAN 6
THE TROUBLE WITH SETTING THE WORLD ON FIRE?

CEDRIC PRICE Let's make the most of it.

JOAN 6
THERE'S ALWAYS SOME GIT WITH A BUCKET OF SAND.

JOAN 3 What's new in the world of visionary buildings?

JOAN LITTLEWOOD
NO ONE KEEPS A DIARY WHEN THEY'RE HAPPY

CEDRIC PRICE Vast swathes of fascinating proposals.

JOAN LITTLEWOOD
STORIES ONLY HAPPEN WHEN YOU'RE SCREWED

CEDRIC PRICE What's new in the world of radical theatre?

JOAN LITTLEWOOD
MISERY'S THE MIDWIFE OF INVENTION

JOAN 3 Tragically little.

JOAN LITTLEWOOD
I CONCLUDE

Music continues, lines overlapping, headlines projected whilst the year counter flicks through the years. **GERRY RAFFLES** *gradually disappears.*

JOAN 1	NOTHING MUCH HAPPENED AFTER THAT/
JOAN 2	WE WERE JUST CHUNTERING ALONG/
JOAN 1	A CLOUDY SKY, A THREAT OF RAIN/
JOAN 2	ANOTHER SCRIPT, ANOTHER PLAY/

JOAN 6   THE TROUBLE WITH
                                SETTING THE WORLD
                                ON FIRE?/
JOAN 1   NOTHING MUCH
                                HAPPENED AFTER
                                THAT/
JOAN 3   AFTER YOU GET WHAT
                                YOU WANT/

JOAN 2   WHILE WE WERE
                                CHUNTERING ALONG/

JOAN 5   THE TROUBLE WITH
                                GETTING YOUR
                                HEART'S DESIRE?

JOAN 3   WHAT DO YOU DO WITH
                                THE WANT?/

JOAN 1   A BROKEN NAIL; A
                                TWINGE OF PAIN/

JOAN 5   CONTENTMENT'S A
                                CONCEPT I DON'T
                                UNDERSTAND/
JOAN 2   TO MY SURPRISE, I HAVE
                                TO SAY/

JOAN 6   THERE'S ALWAYS SOME
                                GIT WITH A BUCKET
                                OF SAND/

JOAN 1	AND THAT WAS FINE.../
JOAN 3	PAT IT AND PRICK IT AND PUT IT AWAY ON A SHELF?/
JOAN LITTLEWOOD	NO ONE KEEPS A DIARY WHEN THEY'RE HAPPY/
JOAN 2	THAT I WAS FINE.../
JOAN 1	FINE./

JOAN 2	FINE./
JOAN 1	THAT WAS FINE./
JOAN 4	THE TRUTH IS: NO MATTER HOW SLYLY OR DEFTLY YOU TRY TO PRETEND/
JOAN LITTLEWOOD	STORIES ONLY HAPPEN WHEN YOU'RE SCREWED/

JOAN 2
SOMEHOW I WAS FINE/

JOAN 1
FINE/

JOAN 2
FINE/

JOAN 1

NOTHING MUCH HAPPENED AFTER THAT/

JOAN 2

WE WERE JUST CHUNTERING ALONG/

JOAN 3

AFTER YOU GET WHAT YOU WANT, WHAT DO YOU DO WITH THE WANT?/

JOAN 4

THE TRUTH IS, NO MATTER HOW SLYLY OR DEFTLY YOU TRY TO PRETEND/

JOAN 5

THE TROUBLE WITH GETTING YOUR HEART'S DESIRE?/

JOAN 6

THE TROUBLE WITH SETTING THE WORLD ON FIRE?/

JOAN LITTLEWOOD

MISERY'S THE MIDWIFE OF INVENTION/

Year counter hits 1975. **ROSALIE** *steps forward.*

ROSALIE It's 1975, Joan. It's time.

JOAN LITTLEWOOD I've barely seen him.

ROSALIE He's gone.

JOAN LITTLEWOOD It got so busy.

ROSALIE It always does. Is this where the story ends?

JOAN LITTLEWOOD The fuck it is. I haven't told him.

ROSALIE Told him what?

JOAN LITTLEWOOD That's Gerry's business. Get him back.

ROSALIE You missed your cue, Joan. He's left the building. You can come back tomorrow, if you like.

JOAN LITTLEWOOD Tomorrow?

ROSALIE Well it's what we do, isn't it?

JOAN LITTLEWOOD What?

ROSALIE Do it again. See him again.

JOAN LITTLEWOOD I don't understand what you're saying.

ROSALIE We never discussed this bit, but we should. The bit that comes afterwards.

JOAN LITTLEWOOD You're a Fury.

ROSALIE I'd love your thoughts. There's your radio work, back at the BBC...

JOAN LITTLEWOOD A harpy.

ROSALIE ...And then there's your subsequent relationship with Baron Philippe de Rothschild...

JOAN LITTLEWOOD You fucking traitor.

ROSALIE Joan—

JOAN LITTLEWOOD Tormenting me with this bile.

ROSALIE Don't play the disingenuous victim, Joan. I told you in Act One: we're only here because of you. I tell you every time. I roll up, night after night – twice on Wednesdays and Saturdays – to serve you and your narcissistic story. And every time, you take your eye off the ball because – well – because that's what you did, isn't it? Is it? Every time.

JOAN LITTLEWOOD I could recast you—

ROSALIE Be. My. Guest. When it comes down to it, Joan, you are a bully who stole people's coats and who may or may not have walked to Manchester.

JOAN LITTLEWOOD And you, Rosalie, are a footnote. And thank you so much for providing me with this much-desired clarity. I won't be requiring your services anymore. Tomorrow, or any other day. So you can fuck off. *(To the* **COMPANY***)* You lot, as well. You're nothing without me – just mouths without voices.

ROSALIE Joan—

JOAN LITTLEWOOD Out!

ROSALIE Did you make the most of him?

The **COMPANY** *leaves the stage, leaving* **JOAN LITTLEWOOD** *alone.*

JOAN LITTLEWOOD It strikes me that life is an exercise in tolerating never being understood.

MUSIC: "CHANGE" – Reprise

(interrupting, to **BAND***)* What the fuck are you playing that for? Do I have to do everything myself? Ok: a rising phrase, followed by a collapse...

MUSIC: "A DECENT DAY" – Introduction

Stick the collapse on the fucking offbeat, would you?

[MUSIC NO. 24: "A DECENT DAY" (Music – vamp starts and undercores speech]

Right. I'll make do with that.

JOAN LITTLEWOOD *is left alone, looking out at the* **AUDIENCE.**

What's the point in changing the world if you're still subject to gravity? The only person who came close to knowing me was Gerry, so I am henceforth unknowable because Gerry can never know the "me" who lost him. You're here: I see that. When I look back on the days Gerry and I spent together, the days we spent apart, do you know which of those days I miss the most? Tomorrow.

[MUSIC NO. 24: SONG: "A DECENT DAY"]

I MET A MAN WHOSE NAME WAS GERRY RAFFLES
WHAT A FUNNY NAME!
HE WAS TALL, AND DARK, AND HANDSOME TOO
WITH A FUNNY NAME
WASN'T HE SPECIAL?

WASN'T HE FINE?
I TOOK HIM ON, THIS MAN CALLED GERRY RAFFLES
TOOK HIM IN MY ARMS
AS WE MADE OUR LIFE, OUR WORK, OUR BED
HE WAS IN MY ARMS
HE WAS A PRINCE
HE WAS A PRINCE
AND I HAVEN'T HAD A DECENT DAY, SINCE
LOVE WAS ELUSIVE
OR CONDITIONAL
NEVER SO REDUCTIVE AS WHEN LOVE ASKED:
'WHOSE SIDE ARE YOU ON?'
LOVE WAS EFFUSIVE
NON-TRADITIONAL
EVER SO INSTRUCTIVE, BUT THEN LOVE SAW A DOOR AND
    WAS GONE, AGAIN
AT FIRST, YOU'RE CONVINCED THAT YOU CAN'T LIVE WITHOUT
    HIM,
THEN DAY, BY DAY GOES BY
YEARS AGO LIVED A MAN CALLED GERRY RAFFLES
WHAT A FUNNY NAME!
GOD, HE WAS SPECIAL;
GOD HE WAS FINE
BUT THEN I WENT AND LOST MY MAN
MY FUNNY NAME, MY PRINCE
AND I HAVEN'T HAD A DECENT DAY, SINCE
NO, NO I HAVEN'T HAD A DECENT DAY, SINCE

Music continues as **JOAN LITTLEWOOD** *begins to exit.*
GERRY RAFFLES *enters and looks around, inquisitively.*

GERRY RAFFLES Hello? I've come about the theatre.

JOAN LITTLEWOOD *doesn't see* **GERRY RAFFLES,** *but
hesitates momentarily before exiting as the lights fade.
Blackout.*

End

PROPS

Littlewood Home
Joke cigarette
Lighter
Thermos flasks
Kitchen Table
School Desk/Kitchen sink
3 x slatted chairs
Littlewood Script
Handbag
Pub bar stool
Door (on wheels)

School
2 x more school desks
2 x WW1 History Text books

Sabotage Birthday
Taste of Honey bed
Sheets
Pillows
Bedding
Final payment envelope
Box of William's Pears
Bedroom dressing

Lyon's Tea Room
Lyons tablecloth
Lyon's waiter tray
Coin purse (with shillings)
2 x Lyon's Tea cups and saucers
Silver teapot
Silver sugar bowl and spoon
Silver milkjug

Paris is a Woman
Paris café table
2 x Paris bentwood chairs
Suitcase
4 x fake cigarettes

Small chestnut branch with flowers
2 x wine glasses
2 x coffee cups and saucers
Small atomiser perfume
String of onions
Waiter's cloth
4 x Paris umbrellas
2 x Paris books
9 x Paris Portrait frames

RADA
Fans x 5
Book/script
Envelope (Regional Repretory letter)
Envelope (Westend letter)
Fountain pen
Cream writing paper
Ballet barre

Journey to Manchester
Letter with train fare to Manchester
Money/cheque
Pens x 2
Cup and Saucer
Address of Archie Harding at the BBC
Dick Whittington bundle (made from a Joan-style skirt)
Dressing for above bundle

BBC Canteen
BBC On Air sign
Tall stool
Smaller stool
2 x plain bentwoods
2 x reporters notepads and pens
1930s headphones
Ham sandwiches (greaseproof paper)
4 x teacups and saucers

111A Grosvener
Tobacco tin
Clipboard with list of "To Dos" (+ pen)

3 x notebooks
2 x research books
2 x rollie cigarettes (cigarette paper and tobacco)

Red Megaphones
Megaphone
2 x scripts/ documents (Red Megaphones)

Miller's Home
Address of abortion clinic

111A Grosvenor St
Cup of tea

Bus
Bus Stop

Emergency Meeting
Letter from Lord Chamberlain

Theatre Workshop Story
Carousel Projector (with slides)

Gerry & Joan
Bunch of Parma Violets
Practical torch
Festival theatre seats
Tickets x 2

Hiroshima & Arts Council
Smyth Report on Hiroshima
Swivel chair
Desk lamp
Paperwork for Arts Council interview
Uranium 235 Script

Pearl Leaves/Babs 1 Arrives
Telephone receivers x 3
Cigarette

Attempted Suicide
Radio
Ashtray
Cigarette stub (fake)
Script (unspecified)
Cup of tea and saucer
Gas Fire
Projection sheet

Stratford East
Railings
Cup of tea
2 x stage brooms
2 x extra plain bentwoods
1 x wooden folding chair
Box with "Jimmie Miller plays 1930-1934" on side
4 x Jimmie Miller scripts
Foolscap folder of documents to sign
Pen
4 x research books
Bag/box of tools & screwdriver
LX tape/period appropriate equivalent
Reel of cable
1950's telephone
Music stand
2 x trombone stands
Violin stand
Shelagh's letter (Postmark Manchester)
Frank's letter (Postmark Soho)
Hal's letter (Postmark NY)
Type writer

Paris Reprise
Cigarello
Lighter
Hotel balcony tray
2 x juice tumblers
2 x coffee cups and saucers
Sugar bowl and spoon
Trick telegram on tray (bursts into flames!)

Hospital

Hospital bed
Hospital sheets
Hospital pillows
Hospital Blanket
Recording of "The Long Long Trail"
Copy of "The Donkeys"
Audition list

Barbara Windsor Audition
Mop & Bucket
Little Bit of Business Score
Notebook

Theatre Workshop Story
Script (unspecified)
2 x umbrellas
13 x hook handled canes
WW1 Gas mask
10 x WW1 reference books
Reel to reel projector and trolley
Conductors baton

Joan & Gerry's apartment
Journal notebook (and pencil)
Joke cigarettes x 2
Script (unspecified) + pencil
7x non-matching teacups
Pen
Glass of brandy
Tray
1960s telephone
1970's telephone

Additional furniture
A Frame Ladder
Taller A frame ladder
2 x small stools (by the vom pillars) with boxes for the teacups
Upright piano
Wicker costume skip

ABOUT THE AUTHOR

Sam Kenyon is a writer, composer, performer and teacher. He has collaborated on work at the RSC (*Vice Versa*, *A Midsummer Night's Dream*, *The Christmas Truce*), Bristol Old Vic (*Swallows & Amazons*), Sheffield Crucible (*Playing For Time*), Cast in Doncaster (*The Glee Club*), Northern Stage (*The Borrowers*, *Close the Coalhouse Door*, *The Glass Slipper*), and The Barbican (*The Firebrand of Florence*). In 2010 he and Erica Whyman co-directed Joan Littlewood's *Oh What a Lovely War* for Northern Stage. As a performer, he worked extensively as an actor-musican with various directors including John Doyle (*Merrily We Roll Along*, *Amadeus* and *Sweeney Todd*). He teaches on the Musical Theatre course at the Royal Academy of Music. In 2005, during rehearsals for Seamus Heaney's *Burial at Thebes* at Nottingham Playhouse he met Murray Melvin, who captivated him with stories about a woman he'd never heard of. Her name was Joan Littlewood. *Miss Littlewood* is his first play.

Lightning Source UK Ltd.
Milton Keynes UK
UKHW020647141022
410433UK00014B/2622